Supernatural Creatures in Arabic Literary Tradition

This volume explores the cultural meaning of several supernatural creatures in Arabia, tracing the historical development of these creatures and their recent representations in the Western world. Utilizing a variety of old and new Arabic, English, and French sources, the text explores creatures including the ghoul and its derivations, the Rukh bird, and the dragon. Unlike other texts, which primarily focus on genies or jinns, this volume explores other supernatural and mythical creatures that have been popular in the Middle East and Arabia for centuries but are less known to Western audiences. Dr. Al-Rawi argues that many of these creatures have pre-Islamic roots, and that they serve an important function in connecting the past with the present, offering a popular vehicle for articulating and imagining the supernatural dimension of existence which helps in consolidating religious views.

Ahmed Al-Rawi is the Associate Professor of News, Social Media, and Public Communication at the School of Communication at Simon Fraser University.

Routledge Focus on Literature

Shakespeare in the Present
Political Lessons under Biden
Philip Goldfarb Styrt

Speech Acts in Blake's *Milton*
Brian Russell Graham

Literature, Education, and Society
Bridging the Gap
Charles F. Altieri

Shakespeare and the Theater of Pity
Shawn Smith

Trauma, Memory and Silence of the Irish Woman in Contemporary Literature
Wounds of the Body and the Soul
Edited by Madalina Armie and Verónica Membrive

Rilke's Hands
An Essay on Gentleness
Harold Schweizer

Orality, Form, and Lyric Unity
Poetics of Michael Donaghy and Don Paterson
Beverley Nadin

Milton and Music
Seth Herbst

Forensic Storytelling and the Literary Roots of Early Modern Feminism
ReSisters
Barbara Abrams

Supernatural Creatures in Arabic Literary Tradition
Ahmed Al-Rawi

For more information about this series, please visit: www.routledge.com/Routledge-Focus-on-Literature/book-series/RFLT

Supernatural Creatures in Arabic Literary Tradition

Ahmed Al-Rawi

NEW YORK AND LONDON

First published 2024
by Routledge
605 Third Avenue, New York, NY 10158

and by Routledge
4 Park Square, Milton Park, Abingdon, Oxon, OX14 4RN

Routledge is an imprint of the Taylor & Francis Group, an informa business

ISBN: 978-1-032-61224-9 (hbk)
ISBN: 978-1-032-61225-6 (pbk)
ISBN: 978-1-003-46263-7 (ebk)

DOI: 10.4324/9781003462637

Typeset in Times New Roman
by Deanta Global Publishing Services, Chennai, India

Contents

Preface

This book explores the cultural meaning of several supernatural creatures in Arabia like the ghoul and its derivations, the Rukh bird, and the dragon. The book traces the historical development of these creatures and some of their recent representations in the Western world. Since the ghoul is much more well known and discussed in the literature, I devoted more space to it in order to elaborately explain the creature's multilayered representation and popular perception.

To support my arguments, I rely on a variety of old and new Arabic, English, and French sources. Instead of focusing on the genies or jinns as many other scholars have elaborately done, I explore in this book other supernatural and mythical animals and creatures that are popular in the Middle East and Arabia but less known to Western audiences, and I argue that many of these creatures have pre-Islamic roots, and that they served an important function in connecting the past with the present. They also offer a popular vehicle for articulating and imagining the supernatural dimension of existence which helps in consolidating religious views.

For a long time, supernatural creatures preoccupied the lives of many people from different cultures and religions. Though their origins are as old as the Mesopotamian civilization, Arabs were largely responsible for popularizing some of them like the ghoul and genies. Because Islam incorporated these beings into its doctrine, some of these supernatural creatures remained a source of fear and mystery in Arab culture. Peter M. Holt and Ann Katherine Holt (1997) argue in *The Cambridge History of Islam* that Islam came about as a "revolt" and as a "protest against" the old Arabs' beliefs, but that it could not change all of their existing convictions. Instead, it "integrated" some old practices such as the yearly pilgrimage to Mecca.

These supernatural beings remain appealing not only to the people in the Middle East region but also to global audiences, mostly because they reflect human concerns about the unknown, offer entertainment and an escape into metaphysical worlds, and elicit fear and imagination.

1 The ghoul[1]

Arabic lexicon

As Arabic is a language very rich in synonyms, several old and standard Arabic lexicons have dealt with the term "ghoul" in different ways. In general, according to these lexicons, the ghoul has a frightening nature and can kill people, especially when they travel. Abu al-Faḍil Ibn Mandhur (1232–1311 CE) in Lisan al-'Arab states that the term "ghoul" stems from a verbal root "ghal" meaning "to kill" (Ibn Mandhur 2005, 2951), and al-'Abad mentions in al-Muhit fi 'l-Lughah that the term ightal, which means "death," was originally derived from the Arabic verb meaning "to murder" (al-'Abad 1994, 130). According to al-Qurtubi, these creatures are thought to delude travelers in the wilderness by confusing them to such an extent that they lose their sense of direction and are driven to perdition (al-Qurtubi 1964, 18). There is thus an etymological mistake in the *Oxford English Dictionary* (1989), which states that "ghoul" is derived from "seize," whereas, as shown above, it stems from the Arabic origin of "ghal" which means "to kill."

According to Abu'l Wafa, a ghoul is "the male genie and the female is called si'lwah, and the plural is 'si'lwahs'" (Ibn Mandhur 2005). But Sa'id bin Ibrahim al-Tasturi (?–971 CE) in *al-Mudhakar wa 'l-Mu'anath* disagrees with this explanation and states that a ghoul is a feminine being, denoting "the enchantress of genies" (al-Tasturi 2001, 42). In addition, al-Jahidh (780–869 CE) noted that "Arabs used to generally refer to the ghoul as a female creature" (al-Jahidh 1969, 195), and Ibn Durayd in *Jamharat al-lughah* (838–933 CE) mentions the term "qutrub" for the male ghoul, a name that also has the meaning "madman" or "drugs" (Ibn Durayd 1987, 1121). Almost 1,000 years later, the English traveler Charles Montagu Doughty (1843– 1926), in his work *Travels in Arabia Deserta* of 1888, referred to an Arab Bedouin who swore that he saw a "ghrôl" or a "ghrul" in the desert, and mentioned that:

> The sex is only feminine, she has a foot as the ass' hoof, and a foot as an ostrich. She entices passengers, calling to them over the waste by their names, so that they think it is their own mother's or their sister's voice.
>
> (Doughty 1933, 53)

DOI: 10.4324/9781003462637-1

Ibn Mandhur is of the opinion that the other meaning of the word suggests the ghoul is one of the "most fearful genies and devils" known to man, since "Arabs used to think that ghouls appear to human beings in the wilderness where they change (yataghawalun) their shapes" (Ibn Mandhur 2005, 2953). In addition, ghoul can mean "the enchantress of genies" since, in the Islamic tradition, devils and genies are thought to be enchanters, a phenomenon also said to be found among human beings in this culture (Ibn Mandhur 2005, 2953). Al-Zubaydi's *Taj 'l-'Arus min Jawahir al-Qamus* mainly repeats interpretations already found in *Lisan al-'Arab*. Al-Zubaydi cites al-Nażir, an Arab lexicographer, in stating that a ghoul is "a devil that devours human beings." In this lexicon, an additional meaning for ghoul is given, that is, a "beast that has fangs." Here the description is connected with Ta'batah Sharran, a well-known Arab poet (al-Zubaydi 1998, 127–33), whose story is narrated below. To sum up, a ghoul in the Arabic language could be defined as a kind of enchanter, a demon of genies, or the devil itself, since there is no agreement on its specific nature. Except for Abu'l-Wafa, who considered the ghoul to be a male genie, most lexicons agree that ghouls were regarded as malicious, ugly male beings – or sometimes female creatures, in the case of si'lwah – with fangs and cloven feet, that were thought to appear to travelers in different shapes in the wilderness. The ghoul is also often described as an ugly female devil that can transform herself into an attractive woman, and it is said she was able to entrance travelers and lead them astray in order to kill them (al-Tahawi 2007, vol. 3, 111).

In order to fully understand the representation of the ghoul found among Arabs, it is necessary to trace this being by referring to narratives and accounts from pre-Islamic and old Arabic texts and oral traditions in order to see the extent to which belief in this supernatural being preoccupied the lives and the imagination of the people in the Arabian region.

The pre-Islamic ghoul

The earliest records of Arabs are found in ancient Iraq – or what is known in the West as Mesopotamia – as cuneiforms provide evidence that the nomads of Arabia were in direct contact with people from neighboring regions for the purpose of trade. This contact produced cultural exchange between the two peoples, in terms of life-style and borrowed words. In ancient Iraq, there was a popular monster called "Gallu" that could be regarded as one of the origins of the Arabic ghoul.[2] Gallu was an Akkadian demon of the underworld "responsible for the abduction of the vegetation-god Damuzi (Tammuz) to the realm of death" (Lindemans, 2008). Since Akkad and Sumer were very close to the Arabian deserts, Arab Bedouins in contact with the culture of ancient Iraq could have borrowed the belief in the ghoul from the Akkadians.

Before discussing different ideas of the ghoul, however, I will examine the ghoul's general depiction in the pre-Islamic context to show that the Arabic ghoul is older than the religion of Islam. In some old Arabic works written before Islam, ghouls were regarded as devilish creatures. al-Mas'udi (c. 896–c. 957), for example, referred in *Muruj al-Dhahab* to the older books written by Ibn 'Ishqq and Wahb Ibn al-Munabbih, who tackled the old Bedouins' myth of creation. Arabs before Islam believed that when God created genies from the gusts of fire, He made from this type of fire their female part, but one of their eggs was split in two. Hence, the Qutrub,[3] which looked like a cat, was created. As for the devils, they came from another egg and settled in the seas. Other evil creatures, such as the Marid,[4] inhabited the islands; the ghoul resided in the wilderness; the si'lwah dwelt in lavatories and waste areas; and the hamah[5] lived in the air in the form of a flying snake (1986, 171).

However, al-Qazwini (c. 1208–c. 1283) mentioned a different description taken from an old Arabic source, which says that when the devils wanted to eavesdrop on Heaven, God threw meteors at them,[6] whereupon some were burnt, fell into the sea, and later turned into crocodiles, while others dropped onto the ground and changed into ghouls (1980, 236). Such descriptions cannot be found in Islamic texts. For instance, Abu 'Uthman al-Jahidh (c. 775–c. 868), who compiled many popular beliefs in his book *al-Haywan* (The Animal), wrote that commoners thought that the devil's eyes were upright, similar to other recent accounts taken from the Bedouins (1969, 214), whose ideas lived on for almost 2,000 years.

Among the earliest stories of those who had an encounter with the ghoul before Islam is that of Ta'bbatah Sharran narrated by Abu'l-Faraj al-Isfahani (897–967 CE) in his book *al-Aghani*. Sharran's real name was Thabit bin Jabir bin Suffyan, and he was said to have had the fastest legs and sharpest eyes imaginable – which helped him greatly when he was hunting gazelles. Consequently, he used to pursue the fastest gazelle, and, if he caught one, he would slaughter it using his sword and he would cook it. One night he encountered a ghoul in a place called Hudhayl and fought against it with his sword until he killed it. After sunrise, he put it under his arm and headed toward his comrades; thereafter, they called him "Ta'bbatah Sharran," meaning "carrying evil under his arm" (al-Isfahani 1983, vol. 21, 146). The poet described the appearance of the ghoul as follows:

> I saw two eyes in an ugly face like the head of a cat, / Having a cloven mouth and / Two deformed legs and a dog's scalp.
>
> (al-Isfahani 1983, 147)

The other story mentioned by al-Isfahani was that of Suffyan, who saw a ram in the desert, so he carried it under his arm after catching him. But the ram kept urinating as he carried him along the road, and his weight increased as Suffyan approached his house. When Suffyan freed the ram, he was surprised to see that it had changed into a ghoul. So, he was later asked: "What did you carry under your arm?" – to which he replied: "evil" (al-Isfahani 1983, 144).

In addition, Umar bin al-Khatab (586–644 CE), the second Muslim Caliph, traveled on one occasion to Syria before the emergence of Islam. After stopping him, a female monster asked the man: "Bin al-Khattab, where are you heading?" The Caliph answered: "This is not your concern," and the ghoul turned its head completely around in order to frighten him (Ibn Mandhur 1990 vol. xxvii, 269–70). Bin al-Khattab noticed that the ghoul had cloven feet just like an ass (al-Manawi 1945, 318). Knowing the evil intentions of the monster, he raised his sword and killed it by striking it between its shoulder and neck. When he returned to the same place after a few hours, however, he could not find the ghoul there (ibid.).

The idea of a fight against a ghoul seems to have been commonly found among the Arab Bedouins. Doughty, for instance, referred to the aga of Kella's description of the "Salewwa." The former believed that she was "nearly like the ghrûl" and described her as "a woman, only she has hoof-feet as the ass" (Doughty 1933, 53). The aga swore that 15 tribesmen once saw her, and, in another incident, 80 men of the Sherarat tribe were said to have encountered her when they lit a fire one evening, "but as their bullets do not her scathe; they took up firebrands to beat the woman-fiend, and they beat on her all that night" (Doughty 1933, 54).

In addition, Abu Asid al-Sa'di mentioned the story of Arqam Bin Abu al-Arqam in which a ghoul appeared and kidnapped al-Arqam's son who was on a desert journey. The ghoul, disguised in the form of a woman, carried the boy on its back. When they saw al-Arqam's friend, the woman pretended to be the boy's attendant (al-Waqidi 1984, 104). This story emphasizes the well-known deceitful and wicked character of the ghoul. In folktales, the motif (G443.2) "ogre abducts woman's children" (El-Shamy 1995, 149) is similar to the account given above. In general, the pre-Islamic ghoul is known as a devilish female creature that intends to inflict harm on travelers and is able to change its form. In most cases, the ghoul is defeated by striking it with a sword.[7] The following section discusses how the ghoul has been associated with Islamic practices.

The Islamic ghoul

When Islam first spread in the Arabian Peninsula in the seventh century, it changed many old customs and beliefs, such as ending the habit of burying recently born baby girls and preventing women from marrying more than one man at a time. It could not, however, change other ideas such as the belief in the ghoul or the si'lwah (si'lah).[8] Prophet Muhammed mentioned the ghoul in several of his sayings, but later Muslim scholars had conflicting views about the authenticity of these sayings, as some negated the ghoul's existence and others confirmed it. Despite the rational voices that rejected the existence of this creature, many Arabs (especially Bedouins) narrated tales and recited poetry that featured or mentioned the ghoul. Since this creature originated in the desert, it has been particularly popular there from the pre-Islamic period to the present day. However, the legend spread to the Arabs' urban areas and became part of the culture ever since, which suggests that the Bedouins' beliefs were very influential, and in some cases formed the very fabric of Arab society. As mentioned earlier, Holt and Holt's argument that Islam could not change all the old beliefs of Arabia is valid in the case of belief in the ghoul and other mythical creatures discussed in this book.

Muhammed himself was said, in many instances, to comment on or confirm the existence of ghouls. For example, Isma'il bin 'Umar Abu al-Fida' (?–c. 1372) mentioned in *Tafsir Ibn Kathir* that ghouls were the "demons of genies," and cited the following famous incident: When the Prophet met his companion Abu Dharr in a mosque, the Prophet advised Abu Dharr to pray in order to be saved from the mischief of the devils of humans and genies. Abu Dharr was surprised to hear the Prophet confirm the existence of creatures such as these, which the Prophet identified as ghouls (1980, 306–8).

In another anecdote, Abu Ayub al-Anşari asked the Prophet's advice because some ghouls were eating from his dates store at night. The Prophet told him to say the following: "In the Name of God, answer the Prophet of God." al-Anşari followed the advice and the ghouls promised not to return. The next day, the Prophet informed the man that the ghouls might come back because they lied. His prediction was accurate. The Prophet then advised al-Anşari to recite the "Ayat al-Kursi" (Throne verse) from the Quran, which proved to be useful in getting rid of the ghouls (Abu al-Fida' 1980, 306–8; al-Tirmidhi n.d., 158; al-Kufi 1988, 94; al-'Asqalani 1959, 159; al-Naysaburi n.d., 519). Abu Asid al-Sa'di, another of the Prophet's companions, had a similar experience (al-'Asqalani 1959, 489) though in this version the ghouls themselves gave advice on how to rid humans of their harm.

To sum up, according to the Prophet of Islam, ghouls are the demons or enchantresses of genies that hurt human beings by eating or spoiling their food and/or by frightening travelers when they are in the wilderness. In order to avoid their harm, one can recite a verse from the Quran or call for prayer since they hate any reference to God.

Other Muslim scholars like Abi al-Sheikh al-Asbahani (c. 887–c. 979) described the ghoul or si'lwah as a kind of a female demon that was able to change its shape and appear to travelers in the wilderness to delude and harm them. He narrated the story of Aḥmed al-Dabbagh's father, who went once on a trip and took a risky road that was known to be frequented by ghouls. After walking for a few hours, Aḥmed al-Dabbagh's father saw a woman wearing a ragged dress lying on a bed above hung lanterns used to illuminate the place. When she saw him approaching, the woman started calling on the man to attract him; however, he realized that she was a ghoul, so he recited the Surat Yasin from the Quran. As a result, the woman put out her lantern lights and said: "Oh man, what did you do to me?" Hence, he was saved from her harm (1987, vol. v, 1652) (Motif F491.10). en-Naddahah, "the she-Caller," was described as a "female spirit who calls people by name and then leads them astray" (El-Shamy 1995, 130).[9]

On the other hand, an authenticated saying attributed to Muhammed by Abdullah Bin Jabir states that ghouls did not exist: "No ghoul, no ʻadwa,[10] and no tayrrah"[11] (Ma'ruf et al. 1996, vol. iv, 251; al-Shawkani 1973, 373; al-Jawhari 1990, 381). In addition to the ghoul, the Prophet negated other fallacies or old customs like the "hama"[12] (al-Ţaḥawi 1994, 308), "banu"[13] (al-Qushayri n.d. 1745; al-Tamimi 1967, 498), "sifr"[14] (Ma'ruf et al. 1996, vol. vi, 23), and "naw"[15] (al-Qushayri n.d. 1742).

Though the sayings attributed to Muhammed seem to contradict one another,[16] many Muslim scholars believe that ghouls used to exist before Islam. For instance, Abu Asid al-Saʻdi (cited above) commented, after narrating a story involving a ghoul, that "ghouls lived at that time [before and at the beginning of Islam], but they perished later" (al-Waqidi 1984, 104). Yusuf al-Hanafi shared the same view, stating that "God could have created this creature, but later He removed its harm from human beings" (n.d., 268). According to the writings of these scholars, Muhammed states ghouls no longer exist because God has rid humans of their mischief. Since Islam clearly dictated that its followers use their rational judgment in assessing matters, there were many Arab writers, particularly those belonging to the al-Muʻtazilah (Recluses) school, who negated the very existence of the ghoul because they relied on reason in analyzing different cultural and religious issues. For instance, al-Jahidh, who was an al-Muʻtazilah member, offered a logical explanation for the myth of the ghoul. He said that if a man sought solitude in the desert, he would be confused, distracted, unfocused, and would start seeing small things as huge. He might also perceive the invisible, hear the inaudible, and view minute matter as utterly magnificent and big (1969, 150). In other words, the desert heat and the fear caused by darkness and loneliness could make any man hallucinate and see illusions. A young person, for instance, who grew up with ghoulish stories that were part of his culture, might go alone to the wilderness in the dead of night and become delusional at the sound of the first owl cries and voice echoes. Sir Richard Burton's interpretation of the ghoul fell along similar lines. In his translation of the "Story of Fourth Voyage of the Es-Sindibad of the Sea" (1886–8, vol. vi, 34–48) in *The Thousand Nights and a Night*, Burton explained the word "Ghul" as "an ogre, a cannibal" and said: "I cannot but regard the 'Ghul of the waste' as an embodiment of the natural fear and horror which a man feels when he faces a really dangerous desert" (1886–8, 36). Finally, Hasan El-Shamy suggests that one's "life space" contains an amalgam of "real" and "imaginary" worlds. "If a child is told that wolves swallow 'kids' whole and live in old tombs, then an association is established between wolves and these acts and objects; for the child, this is what wolves 'really' do" (1999, 7).

al-Jahidh further elaborates by saying that after remembering the hallucination, a man would possibly write poetry or narrate tales about seeing this monster, thus making other people believe in its reality more than before. If that man was a natural liar and habitually exaggerated and overstated matters, he would claim to have seen the ghoul or talked to the si'lwah (1969, 150). Others might pretend that they killed the si'lwah or accompanied it or even married it. al-Jahidh stressed that some of those liars would be tempted to continue misleading others if they encountered naïve commoners who did not question or doubt such tales and who could not distinguish between reality and fantasy (1969, 151). Carl von Sydow classifies such accounts as remembered retellings because they deal with a belief in superstition like stories of ghosts (Green 1997, 92–3), and El-Shamy mentions similar motifs: "origin of jinn [genie]: generated by hallucination caused by sensory deprivation" (A2909) and "hallucinatory experiences from sensory deprivation" (F1043.1) (1995, 58 & 143). In brief, the accounts mentioned above suggest that human beings imagine frightening creatures such as genies and ghouls because of the old fanciful stories they have heard. These supernatural creatures will become more real and will "materialize" when people with feeble minds are frightened or in a state of exhaustion.

Furthermore, the Arab philosopher Abu al-'Ala' al-Ma'arri (c. 973–c. 1057) stated in *Risalat al-Ghufrran* that some Arabs "lied about the ghoul" (1988, 244); he stressed that "whatever was contrary to reason must be a myth" (1988, 223) such as the story of Ta'abbatah Sharran. Another Arab writer who objected to the popular beliefs in the ghoul was al-Jawzi (c. 1116–96). In his book *al-A'dhkya'* (The Bright) al-Jawzi tells the story of a brave and strong man called al-A'drra' in the city of Kufah. al-A'drra' heard once that there was a ghoul near one of the ruins on the outskirts of the city and decided to investigate the matter because he believed that "the devil and the ghoul were only illusions. After riding on his horse at night, he suddenly saw a fiery creature decreasing and increasing in its size. As the horse panicked, the man was forced to walk, and he followed the trace of fire to a cellar located under the ruins. The man felt his way along the narrow corridors because it was very dark, and when he reached its end, he caught a person. Astonished, al-A'drra' found out that the fiery shape was only a black woman, so he swore to kill her if she would not speak the truth. Instead, the woman asked a question: "Are you a genie or a human being? I have never seen anyone else braver than you!" The man discovered that the lady was a slave serving a family in Kufah who ran away and stayed in the ruins. In order to survive, the woman had the idea of terrifying travelers by using a stick, a candle, and a piece of cloth. She used to hold the candle in one hand and the stick in another and place the piece of cloth over the stick. By moving them all, she managed to create an illusion of a glittering indistinct creature. Then she would do the same without the stick to fool the people by showing that the creature changed its size. For two decades the woman was able to use this same trick to frighten travelers, who would drop their luggage and run away. After learning her story, the man took the woman to her owners, and travelers were harmed no more by the alleged ghoul (2001, 107).

In brief, conflicting views about the existence of ghouls imply that Muslim scholars were still struggling to balance the widespread popular beliefs from the Jahiliyya era (before Islam) with the new rational interpretations of the Islamic doctrine. In order to understand the further influence of the ghoul on Arab culture, this chapter will analyze the popular beliefs expressed in different accounts from the Arabic oral tradition after the emergence of Islam.

Arabic culture

Arab Bedouins believed in different mythic beings, including the ghoul, and they thought that this creature inhabited the desert, a highly desolate area where the imagination played a very important role in people's experience of the being. As a matter of fact, there are several stories to be found in Arabic culture that involve an encounter with, or a fight against, a ghoul. Also, early Arabic culture is mainly reflected in the oral tradition and literary works, especially poetry. However, there were other outlets by which writers expressed their views of their culture such as books of history, science, and philosophy.

The Arab encyclopedic writer al-Jahidh wrote about the types of animals and other creatures in *al-Haywan*. He said the ghoul was believed to attract travelers by setting fires at night; subsequently, the travelers would lose their sense of direction (Motif G0412.3 "ogre's (ogress's) fire lures person") (El-Shamy 2004, 1073). As mentioned above, al-Jahidh elaborated by saying that people viewed the ghoul as a type of genie, and the si'lwah was the female genie if she did not change (tataghawal) or become a ghoul and delude travelers. If a genie changed its shape and harassed travelers, it would become a she-devil or ghoul (1969, 195). In fact, al-Jahidh confirmed the continuous belief in the ghoul and added a strange conviction popular among Arabs: the si'lwah would die only by one mighty blow from a sword because if two strikes were directed to it, it would not expire until 1,000 blows followed (1969, 233 and 235). The same belief is still found in current folktales from the Arab region, for the same one-strike reference is found in one of the folktales collected by Muhawi and Kanaana (1989, 65). On the other hand, Yusuf Ibn 'Abdulbar al-Qurtubi (c. 978–c. 1071) considered the abovementioned view one of the Arab Bedouins' legends, and the author harshly criticized al-Jahidh for citing such a popular belief and accused him of being "foolish" (1982, 177). Nevertheless, this belief was widespread. The best example is probably found in the *Arabian Nights*, which contains many other popular convictions dating back to medieval times (Perho 2004; Shosha 2004). Also, Silvestre de Sacy stresses that there are Islamic elements in the composition of the *Arabian Nights* (Sadan 2004, 44). When Antoine Galland first translated the *Arabian Nights* into a European language, he mentioned in the preface that the stories "must be pleasing, because of the account they give of the Customs and Manners of the Eastern Nations" (1718, "Preface"). Furthermore, Lady Mary Wortley Montagu (1689–1762) compared the strange scenes and items found in Turkey with what she read in the "Arabian Tales." Montagu reminded her sister by saying: "You forget … those very tales were written by an author of this country, and (excepting the enchantments) are a real representation of the manners here" (1992, 157). Despite the fact that the *Arabian Nights* was only a fictitious work, Galland and Montagu considered it an accurate representation of Islamic culture instead of viewing it as a receptacle of some popular old beliefs.

There was also the story of Marwan bin Hafsah, who once stated that he and his fellows went to Harun al-Rashıd, the Arab Caliphate, and walked through a desolate area. When night fell, a woman appeared and followed them to attend to their camels. "She was the ghoul herself." But at dawn, she turned away saying: "Oh thou morning star, keep away from me / As I neither belong to you nor you to me." Hafsah stated that he had never felt as frightened in his whole life as he had on that occasion (al-Isfahanı 1983, vol. 10, 99).

Generally speaking, stories in Arabic culture that contain the motif of a fight occurring between a human being and a ghoul usually represent the ghoul as an ugly female creature seeking to harm others. Typically, the fight involves striking the monster with a sword and ends with victory over the ghoul. On the other hand, there are some stories in which the ghoul shows no signs of being a dangerous or threatening being. Instead, it befriends humans and even marries some of them. Ibrahim al-Bayhaqi (?–932 CE), for example, cited a story narrated by Abu Zayd al-Nahwi in which a si'lwah lived for a time among the tribe of Bani Tamim, until it gave birth to a baby ghoul. But one day it saw lightning coming from the land of si'lwahat, so it started to feel homesick and headed at once toward its old comrades (al-Jahidh 1969, 186; al-Bayhaqi 1984, 104). In the same context, 'Abdullah al-Bakri (1040–94 CE) stated that an Arab called Umrubin Yarbu' bin Handalah helped a si'lwah to give birth (al-Bakrı 2001, 1240); however, al-Jahidh mentioned that Yarbu' actually married this si'lwah who, after begetting a few sons, ran away when it saw lightning and remembered its homeland (al-Jahidh 1969, 186 and 197). The story narrated by al-Bayhaqi was probably the same as the one mentioned by al-Bakri and al-Jahidh, but it lacked the details provided by them.

In addition, Yaqut al-Hamawi (1178–1229) said that Khalid bin Yazid, an Arab literary figure, claimed that he knew someone called Abu Sulayman who slept in the wilderness with the ghoul and actually married the si'lwah (al-Hamawi 1988, 44). al-Jahidh himself devoted a whole section of his book *al-Haywan* to alleged marriages between humans and genies (al-Jahidh 1969, 196–8). Furthermore, Westermarck, writing in the nineteenth century, observed that many Moors or Arabs used to believe in the reality of marriages taking place between genies and human beings (Westermarck 1899, 252,

253 and 260), and in the second half of the twentieth century, Crapanzano mentioned how Arabs in Morocco thought that some genies were actually married to some of their men (Crapanzano 1985, 101).

Other writers, such as Kamalludin al-Dimiri (1341–1405 CE), mentioned that the ghoul was thought to change its shape. He was citing the famous Arab poet, Ka'ab bin Zuhayr, who wrote: "No condition lasts forever, for it changes like the changing shape of the ghouls" (al-Dimiri 1978, vol. 2, 134). Genies, just like ghouls, where also thought to be capable of shape-shifting.[17] In the same context, al-Dimiri said that the ghoul was also called "Khayt'aur" referring to "anything that does not stay in the same condition and fades away like a mirage" (al-Dimiri 1978, vol. 2, 134). Similarly, al-Jahidh mentioned that the common people believed that genies, devils, and ghouls had the ability to transform themselves into whatever forms they liked. However, even though it could change into the shape of a beautiful woman, the ghoul's legs would remain like those of an ass (al-Jahidh 1969, 114 and 120), an idea also emphasized by Raghib al-Isfahani (al-Isfahani 2004, 609). In addition, Abu Umar Yusif al-Nimri (977–1071 CE) mentioned in al-Tamhid li Ibn 'Abdulbar that a ghoul and a si'lwah were one and the same creature.

Sometimes ghouls become inflated and large and at other times they get smaller, and change from being ugly to being beautiful. At times, they wear the visage of a human being and at other times that of an animal, and change by their own will (al-Nimri 1976, 268). It should also be mentioned that al-Jahidh drew attention to a conviction among Arabs that the si'lwah would only die by one mighty blow from a sword. If 2 blows were directed a it, it would never die until 1,000 blows followed (al-Jahidh 1969, 233 and 235). This belief was widespread in the Arabic world and remained alive in folktales. It was mentioned, for instance, in Richard Burton's translation of the "Story of Prince Sayf Al-Muluk and the Princess Badi'a Al-Jamal" (ATU 1137: The blinded ogre [Uther 2004]; E11.1: Second blow resuscitates. First kills [Thompson 1956]) in *The Thousand Nights and a Night* (Burton 1886–8). In this story, a man and his companions were taken by a ghoul to its cave but managed to blind its eyes with a hot spit and to smite it with "the sword, a single stroke across his waist." Then the ghoul cried out: "O man, thou desire to slay me, strike me a second stroke." As the man was about to hit it again, his companion said: "Smite him not a second time, for then he will not die, but will live and destroy us" (Burton 1886–8, vol. 7, 361). This story had the same theme as that of "Fatma the Beautiful" (mentioned later) since Fatma and Sa'id were about to be deceived by the ghoul, but before being devoured by it they managed to kill it by means of a trick.

In addition to the abovementioned accounts, al-Abshihi gave another description of the ghoul. He said that it looked like a very ugly beast in which were combined some features of a human being. It was an ill-omened animal that could not be tamed by human beings, so it became wild and sought the wilderness. Human beings might faint upon seeing a ghoul, and only a few strong people could withstand its ugliness and remain unaffected (al-Abshihi 1983, 177). al-Abshihi borrowed al-Dimiri's description of the si'lwah, saying that it was a devilish beast that appeared to people during the day but changed into a ghoul at night. The former added that it was usually seen near water springs and fountains (al-Abshihi 1983, 286). Similarly, Westermarck mentioned how "Aisha Kandisha" was believed to dwell in wells, rivers, and the sea (Westermarck 1899, 259), and Lady Duff-Gordon Lucie (1821–69), a British woman who visited Egypt in 1864, described in her *Letters from Egypt* (Gordon 1902) how she had heard about the ghoul from some natives. In a letter sent to her mother, Mrs. Sarah Austin, on February 19, 1864, she stated that Sand had invited her and a friend called Mustapha into the desert, to view a well: "There is a Roman well in his yard with a ghoul in it. I can't get the story from Mustapha, who is ashamed of such superstitions, but I'll find it out" (Gordon 1902, 120). Finally, in the Arabic version of the *Arabian Nights*, Jahinshah and his companions lost their way at sea and found an island. When they went to it, they started walking and found a man sitting beside a well. The man, who happened to act like a ghoul, talked, and afterwards only whistled like a bird. He then divided himself into two, and then again into four parts, with each part wanting to eat the travelers (Alf Layla wa Layla n.d., vol. 3, 71–2, "Four Hundred and Eighty-Nine Nights"). The two writers al-Abshihi and al-Dimiri further clarify the nature of the Qutrub mentioned above by referring to it as a devilish male creature that appears near the outskirts of Yemen and at the Nile Delta. It is believed to follow human beings in order to frighten them or to mate with them, and to lead ultimately to their death. According to these writers, if the ghoul only frightened the person, his condition would be cured by being calmed down; however, if sexual intercourse took place, the person's fate was sealed (al-Dimiri 1978, vol. 12, 219; al-Abshihi 1983, 178).[18]

Indeed, the *Arabian Nights* abound with references to the ghoul and some of the ideas cited above. For instance, Richard Burton's translation of the "Story of Prince Sayf Al-Muluk and the Princess Badi'a Al-Jamal" in *The Thousand Nights and a Night*, which is cited above, corresponds with al-Jahidh's account of how to kill a ghoul by striking it once; apparently such a belief had not faded away from Arabic culture despite the fact that many centuries elapsed between al-Jahidh's time and that of the *Arabian Nights* composition. Muhsin Mahdi confirms that certain story tellers of the *Arabian Nights* transformed some anecdotes found in the books of history into fiction. For instance, al-Mas'udi recorded an account similar to the tale of "The Hunchback and the King of China" in the *Arabian Nights* (1995, 165–6). The following tale further suggests the link between factual written accounts and fictional tales.

In a story cited by al-Asbahani and narrated by Zaid Bin A'slam, two men from Ashjja tribe "wanted to provide a bride with her wedding outfits, so they went on a trip to an area where they saw a lonely woman. Upon seeing them, the woman said: "What is your need?"; the men replied, "We want to provide a bride with her needs." The woman said she could assist in this business if the two men promised to come back to her, so they made a promise. When they finished their business, the two men returned to the lady. She said: "I will follow you in your journey." They made her ride on one of their camels until they reached a sand mound where the woman stopped and said: "I have some business here," suggesting that she wanted to relieve herself. Unexpectedly, the woman remained behind the mound for an hour; thus, one of the two men went to check, yet he was delayed, too. When the other man climbed the mound and looked, he was shocked to see that the woman was lying on the man's belly and eating his liver. As a result, the man ran as fast as possible to escape from this woman, but she glimpsed him and followed his path. After stopping him, she said: "What is wrong with you?"; he replied: "There is an iniquitous devil among us." Despite the harm she inflicted on the other man, the woman gave advice on how to avoid her mischief by supplicating and mentioning God. The moment the man did what he was advised, a fire fell from the sky and ripped the woman in two, so he thanked God for killing the si'lwah (1987, vol. v, 1671–2). This tale is somewhat similar to the tales of the "King's Son and the Ogress" and "The Tale of the King's Son and the She-Ghoul" (Haddawy 1992, 42–55) in the *Arabian Nights*, which further suggests that some tales in the *Arabian Nights* are more or less derived from written texts. The idea that ghouls could be driven away by reciting verses from the Quran persisted for a long time because it was recommended by the Prophet, as previously explained. In fact, such an idea is borrowed from Abu Asid al-Sa'di's account and other anecdotes involving the Prophet. For instance, Gharib, the character in Richard Burton's translation of the story "The History of Gharib and His Brother Ajib" in *The Thousand Nights and a Night*, was caught by a ghoul. He started crying God's name and supplicating. As a result, Gharib was able to release himself from the ghoul's grip and finally killed it (1886–8, vol. vi, 257–95). The motifs in this tale are similar to those in the one narrated by Aḥmed al-Dabbagh's father cited above, which gives an idea of the possible source of this *Arabian Nights* tale. In general, the moral of such tales is to show God's supremacy, which is far beyond the power of this naïve monster. In addition, there is a recurrent notion that ghouls show up along desolate roads asking for help. They usually ask for a ride on a camel or horse with other passengers until they reach a proper place to stop and carry out their hideous plans.

Another popular and cultural aspect of the ghoul is the belief that it can change its shape; for instance, Antoine Galland translated a tale from the *Arabian Nights* entitled "The Story of the Vizier That Was Punished" (1798, 77–9), in which an ogre or the Western equivalent of the si'lwah explains: "The Lady was a Hogres, wife to one of those Savage Demons, called Hogres, who stay in remote places, and make use of a thousand wiles to surprise and devour passengers" (1798, 78). The portrayal of the ogre in this story is similar to the typical Arabic cultural concept of the ghoul that changes its shape and usually becomes an attractive woman in order to kill human beings. Again, al-Jahidh referred to this trait of the ghoul in his book *al-Haywan*, as mentioned earlier.

Other fallacies about the ghoul that are also referenced above include the belief that it has "cloven feet similar to that of a goat," according to al-Mas'udi (1986, 170), or closer to those of an "ass" (al-Manawi 1945, 318). There was also the cultural practice of hanging a paw of a rabbit around one's neck for protection from the offenses of genies and the evil fires of the si'lwah (al-Isfahani 2004, 316–7). Furthermore, Arabs believed that ghouls resided on islands, for instance, al-A'drisi (c. 1100–c. 1166) mentioned that there was an island called "the si'ali" (she-ghouls) where certain creatures that looked like women lived, having long fangs and bright eyes like lightning. There was no difference between the males and females except for their genitals and their dress, which was made of tree leaves (1866, 53). Furthermore, Ibn Sa'id al-Maghribi (c. 1213–c. 1286) said that there were almost 100 small islands called "the ghoul" wherein black naked people lived and spoke an indistinct language (1970, 130). In the *Arabian Nights*, many references to the ghoul correspond with the above description. For instance, Lane and Burton narrated the "Story of Fourth Voyage of the Es-Sindibad of the Sea" (Lane 1865, 35–49; Burton 1886–8, vol. vi, 34–48) in which Sindibad traveled from Basrah and saw many islands, but nearly drowned when he was shipwrecked. Sindibad managed to swim with some of his comrades to an island by using a plank from the ship. On the shore, they saw a high building and walked toward it. Standing near the gate, a group of naked savage men ran toward them and took them all to the king. Those naked men were the "Magian people" and their king was a "Ghul" (1886–8, 36). Whoever came to their island was required to eat a certain kind of food, but unlike his fellows, whose minds were "stupefied" and "became changed," Sindibad could not eat. Then Sindibad's fellows were given coconut oil until they became very fat and stupid after which they were roasted and presented to the king. However, Sindibad succeeded in escaping after learning that the Magians eat raw human flesh.

Finally, the ghoul was thought to have magical powers by possessing human bodies. Some Western travelers to Arabia in the nineteenth century documented such a popular conviction;[19] for example, in *Personal Narrative of a Pilgrimage to Al-Madinah and Meccah* (1893), Sir Richard Burton pointed out that Arab Bedouins followed traditional medical practices based on superstitions because they interpreted rabies as: "a bit of meat [that] falls from the sky, and that a dog eating it becomes mad." If a man was bitten by such a dog, his fellows must "shut him up with food, in a solitary chamber, for four days"; however, if he continued barking like a dog, they would "expel the Ghúl (demon) from him, by pouring over him boiling water mixed with ashes" (1893, 389). In other words, the Bedouins believed that the ghoul could possess a man's body and make him mad. To this day, many Arabs believe that genies can take over a man's body if he does not practice his religion in a proper way; hence, violent means are used by the cleric to exorcize the evil spirit. In her study of popular Islam (unorthodox religious practices), Gerda Sengers mentions the zar as an exorcizing ritual well known in Egypt in modern times. The jinn (genies) and asyad (demons) are believed to be responsible for "clothing" (possessing) one's body, and the main method of driving these supernatural beings away from the body is by reciting certain verses from the Quran (2003, 23–4). On the other hand, in Burton's account, Arab Bedouins think of the ghouls as a kind of genie that possesses one's body instead of being an animal-like creature, denoting that this monster has retained its old ethereal character mentioned in Islamic texts.

It is important here to refer to similar ghoul descriptions as found in other Western travelers' accounts. Edward Westermarck, who was a nineteenth-century English traveler, for example, noted the ideas that Moroccans held about genies:

> The Moors … believe in the existence of beings named ġuál (sing. ġôl), who have black faces and eyes like flaming fire, and are fond of human flesh. There are, however, no ġuál in Morocco. They live only in the Sudan, and in Morocco one hears of them chiefly from mothers who want to frighten their children. I have heard some people say that the ġuál are not ġnûn, but form a species by themselves, whereas others are of opinion that they belong to the g˙ inn-kind.
>
> (Westermarck 1899, 259)

The description Westermarck gives is akin to that of a si'lwah dealt with above. Furthermore, his mention of the use of the genie, in Moroccan tradition, as a bogeyman to frighten children, is echoed in the admonition that many children in Arabic countries, such as Iraq, Palestine, and Yemen, still get from their mothers or grandmothers, that is, not to go out in the street or do naughty things, lest the si'lwah should come and take them to her hideout.

Westermarck also claimed that a she-ghoul called "Aysha Qandisha" was afraid of iron and was well known throughout Morocco. He further clarified the nature of this creature, saying:

> She appears in various shapes, now as a child, now as a grown-up woman, with long hair and a beautiful face, but with the legs of a goat or an ass. She knows the name of every man; but when she calls anybody he should not answer her, for she is very dangerous. Not only does she kill men, she is, also, sometimes said to eat them.
>
> (Westermarck 1899, 259)

After several decades, Vincent Crapanzano, in his study of Hamadsha, an Islamic brotherhood, confirmed that belief in ghouls was still a "peripheral" or "fringe phenomenon" in Moroccan society (Crapanzano 1973, 7). He mentioned that the common people used to fear Lalla 'A'isha Sudaniyya, who was the "most powerful of all jinniyya" (Crapanzano 1985, 101). Crapanzano witnessed how people in Morocco used to dance in order to enter into a trance to satisfy ʻAysha Qandisha, the she-devil, who had taken possession of them (2003, 67). ʻAysha Qandisha's manifestations included other she-devils like "Lalla Aisha Dghugha, Lalla Aisha Gnawiyya, and Lalla Aisha Hasnawiyya" (Crapanzano 1985, 98). Crapanzano elaborated on this by giving the following account, which resembles that of Edward Westermarck:

> A man is walking along a road, and suddenly his vision blurs. He thinks there is something wrong with his eyes, but in fact it is Lalla Aisha Hansnawiyya. He sees only her in front of him, and he looks on and sees only her. When he comes to an isolated crossing or path, she takes him by the hand. She asks him why he is following her and where he knows her from. The man tries to excuse himself and says that he thought she was a woman he knew. She says, "Fine. Welcome. Come with me."
>
> (Crapanzano 1973, 144)

Apart from the abovementioned old and recent oral tradition tales, many comparisons were made in Arabic poetry between ghouls and human beings in order to describe an ugly woman, a forceful man, or an evil trait. For instance, ʻAşim Bin Kharwaʻah al-Nahshali disparaged his wife saying:

> She is the ghoul and the devil put together…,
> Whoever accompanies the ghoul and the devil is depressed,
> Even genies seek God's protection upon seeing her.
>
> (Hashim 2001, 813)

The ghoul was used in many Arab proverbs to denote different meanings; for instance, it referred to a repulsive human being with a horrible-looking face: "Uglier than a monkey, uglier than a pig, uglier than a ghoul" (al-Naysaburi, 129) or "uglier than the devil," which referred sometimes to the ghoul's repulsiveness (al-Jawzi 1983, 63). al-Qazwini pointed out that Arabs stressed the ghoul's ugly features. However, even if they did not see a ghoul, mentioning its name in poetry and tales brought fear to listeners (1980, 387).

In brief, the Arabs understood the ghoul to be an ugly female demon that intended to harm travelers and even kill them in some cases. It has the ability to change its form and become a beautiful woman to attract men or even to mate with them. The ghoul's description is close to that of a predatory animal that has fangs and cloven feet, and combines features of the snake, goat, and ass.

Arab oral tradition

Regarding the Arabic oral tradition, numerous folktales deal with the ghoul, especially with the siʻalwah. These tales depict the monster in the same manner mentioned above. In the following section, examples of Arabic folktales incorporating the ghoul are given.

Ibrahim Muhawi and Sharif Kanaana, in *Speak Bird, Speak Again: Palestinian Arab Folktales*, cite several Palestinian folktales in which the ghoul is mentioned. "Precious One and Worn-Out" (Muhawi and Kanaana 1989, 63–6), for instance, deals with a boy who was guarding his father's animal pen because many sheep had disappeared. After spending a few hours in the pen, the boy saw a ghoul stealing a sheep and taking it to a well where it used to hide. After volunteering to go down the well, the boy discovered three beautiful captive girls in it, and he swore that he would kill the ghoul in order to rescue them. When the ghoul returned, the boy managed to strike it on its neck, but the monster urged him to "strike again" (Muhawi and Kanaana 1989, 65). Finally, the boy succeeded in saving the girls. This story could be linked to the ones mentioned above as the ghoul asked the boy to strike a second time, a remark related to the popular belief that ghouls live if struck more than once.

On the other hand, Muhawi and Kanaana refer to other folktales, such as "Little Nightingale the Crier" (1989, 103–12), "The Brave Lad" (1989, 149–51), "The Old Woman Ghouleh" (1989, 176–8), "Clever Hasan" (1989, 189–99), and "The Ghouleh of Trans-Jordan" (1989, 235–8), and so on, some of which contain a ghoul or a ghouleh (a female ghoul) who helps human beings by guiding them in order that they might reach their goals. Similarly, Inea Bushnaq translated several examples of Arabic folktales in *Arab Folk Tales* (Bushnaq 1986) and included an Egyptian tale entitled "The Nightingale That Shrieked" (1986, 89–94), and a Syrian tale called "The Bird of the Golden Feather" (19896, 80–8), which deal with friendly ghouls who assist humans while they are on their journeys. Such tales describe the ghoul as a friendly creature who allies itself with human beings, just as it was said to do in the older tales of Umrubin Yarbu‘ bin Handalah and Khalid bin Yazid.

In addition, Ahmed Shahi and F.C.T. Moore collected several stories from Arabic folklore in their work *Wisdom from the Nile* (Shahi and Moore 1978), including a Nubian tale entitled "Fatma the Beautiful." It dealt with seven girls who once went into the wilderness to collect firewood. When they saw fire from afar, they followed it, and the girls were caught by an ogress[20] as the fire had been deliberately made in order to attract their attention. When the ogress disclosed her intention to feed her seven children with the seven captive girls, Fatma realized the danger surrounding her, and she was able to deceive the ogress and run away with her sisters. In the end, the ogress was killed by a crocodile because of Fatma's scheming (Shahi and Moore 1978, 125–6).

Salih Bin Hamadi collected several folktales from Tunisia and included a story entitled "Muhala," which was also the name of the heroine (Hamadı 1983, 196–200). It essentially followed the description found in "Fatma the Beautiful." Muhala's friends were killed by the ghoul because they did not listen to her advice to refrain from drinking milk offered by a monster (compare D1367.6: Magic food causes insanity [Thompson 1956]) – a somewhat similar motif is to be found in other Arabic tales such as the "Story of the Fourth Voyage of the Es-Sindibad of the Sea" in the *Arabian Nights* (Lane 1865, 35–49; Burton 1886–78, vol. 6, 34–48).

Finally, 'Abdul Qadir al-Baghdadi (c. 1620–c. 1682) cited the Arab poet Kamil, who wrote: "After viewing the fellows of my age, I found no true friend who could stand by you at times of need / I have known then that the impossible matters are three: the ghoul, the phoenix, and a faithful friend" (1979, 136). These lines of poetry have become proverbial in Arabic, which suggests that many Arabs believe that the existence of the ghoul is a mere illusion.

In brief, rational interpretations of the fallacy of the ghoul verify that many Arabs wanted to uncover the nature of this monster to enlighten the people in order that they not be deceived by popular tales. After discussing the ghoul in Arabic lexicon, culture, and oral tradition culture, I will now examine the question of when this monster crossed the desert borders to the West, and what other dreadful features it has been given that have made it a source of inspiration and fear for many people across the globe.

The ghoul's Western transformation

As mentioned above, the ghoul is considered as a kind of devilish genie and was part of the beliefs held by Arabs long before the advent of Islam. Throughout different historical and religious periods, the character of the ghoul remained the same, being represented as an ugly human-like monster that dwelt in the desert and secluded locations, in order to delude travelers by lighting a fire and thus leading them astray. In some cases, this creature was said to have killed travelers. I argue here that when Antoine Galland translated the *Arabian Nights* into French (12 volumes, 1704–17) he took liberties with the Arabic ghoul by representing it as a frightening creature feasting on corpses in cemeteries (see *Arabian Nights Entertainments* 1718, vol. 11, 78–91, "The Story of Sidi Nouman"). For example, Galland emphasized that the ghoul used to dig graves and eat corpses if it needed food, an idea that was never mentioned in any of the Arabic sources. Accordingly, numerous English writers followed Galland's description and further fantasized in their works about the viciousness of this creature. In another section of this chapter, I argue that one of the possible influences on Charles Perrault's *Le Petit Poucet* folktale is Galland himself, notably his introduction of the ghoul figure to the story.

In an attempt to trace the original source of the ghoul in Western thought, one has to investigate some of the earliest Western references to it, one of which can be found in Barthelemy d'Herbelot's (1625–95) *Bibliothéque orientale, ou Dictionnaire universel, contenant tout ce qui fait connaître les peuples de l'Orient* (Herbelot 2001 [1697]). This is considered to be the first encyclopedia of Islam written in a European language. In fact, Antoine Galland worked as an assistant to d'Herbelot, and he actually edited the volumes of the encyclopedia on his own after d'Herbelot's death. In this work, the "Goul" and the "Afriet" are described as the most frightening kind of "Ginns" (d'Herbelot 2001, vol. 5, 193), but no further details are given about ghouls.

Later, when Galland first translated the *Arabian Nights* into the French language, as *Les Mille et Une Nuits* (12 volumes), he depended on a Syrian manuscript that he worked on between 1704 and 1717. The tales in the first eight volumes were taken from this Arabic manuscript, whereas those in the remaining parts (volumes 9 to 12), being without Arabic originals, are called the "orphan tales"; that is, they were mainly taken from other sources, such as oral tales. Many scholars now believe that a Maronite Syrian called Yuhanna or Hanna Diyab met Galland during his visit to Paris in 1709, and helped him in many ways to compose stories such as "Ali Baba and the Forty Thieves," "The Story of Sidi Nouman," and "Aladdin" (Haddawy 1992, xvii; Mahdi 1995, 32; Larzul 2004, 258; Marzolph & van Leeuwen 2004, vol. 2, 582–3). Galland added some stories of his own in order to satisfy the reading public that eagerly awaited the publication of each volume, as well as to compete with another translator, François Pétis de la Croix, who translated into French some *Arabian Nights* tales from the Turkish language (Larzul 2004, 260). Mahdi has noted that Galland's translation is now considered "an outstanding work of eighteenth-century French prose" (1995, 35), because of the unrelated details added by the translator. As Haddawy observed, Galland "deleted, added, and altered drastically to produce not a translation, but a French adaptation" (Haddawy 1992, xx) of the *Arabian Nights*. In light of this, it is important to examine Galland's description of the ghoul.

In Galland's "The Story of Sidi Nouman"[21] (*Arabian Nights Entertainments* 1718, vol. 11, 78–91), whose "Arabic version has never been found" (Marzolph & van Leeuwen 2004, vol. 1, 380), a married man narrated his experience with his wife, Amina. He complained that she did not eat well after their marriage and that she preferred to take just a few grains of rice:

> [M]y wife, instead of making use of a spoon, pulled a little case out of her pocket, and took out of it an ear-picker, with which she picked up the rice grain by grain.
>
> (*Arabian Nights Entertainments*, 1718, vol. 11, 79)

The husband discovered later that his wife was an enchantress accompanying a ghoul. According to the man, ghouls "of both sexes are wandering demons, which generally infest old buildings, from whence they rush, but by surprise, on people that pass by, kill them, and eat their flesh" (*Arabian Nights Entertainments* 1718, vol. 11, 81). Until this point, the description of the ghoul matches that found in other accounts mentioned in the different Arabic sources cited above, but the man continues his portrayal, saying that ghouls in "want of prey, will sometimes go in the night into burying grounds, and feed upon dead bodies that have been buried there" (*Arabian Nights Entertainments* 1718, vol. 11, 81).[22]

In fact, ghouls depicted as male creatures residing in graveyards and eating corpses do not appear to be mentioned anywhere in the Arabic language, literature, culture, or folktales,[23] which seems to indicate that Galland added this detail himself in order to give a more horrific and exaggerated description of the ghoul. In his translation, Galland even added a note explaining the meaning of the word, saying: "Goule, ou goul: ce sont, suivant la religion mahométane, des génies dévorant les cadavres des cimetières" (Galland 1949, 186).[24] It seems that Galland not only changed the meaning of Arabic words but also took great liberties with his translation.

According to W.F. Kirby, "The Story of Sidi Nouman" as found in Galland cannot be authentic because: "the feast of the Ghools is … Greek or Turkish, rather than Arabic, in character, as vampires personified plague, and similar horrors are much commoner in the folk-lore of the former peoples" (Kirby 1886, 466).

The above opinion may well be valid in view of this discussion, and also because of the fact that Galland could have read the story as he "could and did easily read and translate Ottoman Turkish and Persian" (Mahdi 1995, 14). He could also have heard the story in Turkey as he stayed "in Istanbul while serving there as an assistant to the French ambassador to the Ottoman Empire" (Beaumont 2002). Additionally, he sent the Beyânî manuscript (1636) – the only surviving Turkish translation of the manuscript of the *Arabian Nights*, in ten volumes – to France. It is, of course, possible that the Turkish translator of the Beyânî manuscript might have taken "certain liberties with regard to the [Arabic] original," and could have added some details of his own in relation to the ghoul, and later Galland might have depended on him in his interpretation of this creature (Birkalan 2004, 225).

According to the *Oxford English Dictionary*, the word "ghoul" nowadays means an "evil spirit supposed (in Muslim countries) to rob graves and prey on human corpses" (1989). This inaccuracy is clearly an effect of Galland's translation, which was not a faithful rendition of the Arabic original word. Unfortunately, other works followed Galland's new description of the ghoul without further inquiry. For instance, the famous orientalist William Lane (1801–76) suggested the ghoul "applied to any cannibal," as a creature that "appear[ed] in the forms of various animals, and in many monstrous shapes" so as to "haunt burial-grounds and other sequestered spots; [and] … feed upon dead human bodies" (1987, 42; 1860, 227). This description corresponded with Galland's account. Lane did not cite any Arabic reference to support his claim; instead, he referred to Galland's translation of the *Arabian Nights* rather than original Arabic sources. Lane also contradicted his own work because he never described the ghoul in such a manner in his book *An Arabic-English Lexicon*, in which numerous Arabic references were used (1980, 2311).[25] Furthermore, in his excellent classification of Arab folktales, Hasan

El-Shamy mentioned motif G20 "Ghouls. Persons eat corpses" and its subtypes by referring to Victor Chauvin (1995, vol. i, 144). However, the latter only cited Galland's "Sidi Nouman" tale as evidence of his claim (1902, vol. vi, 198). As in Lane's case, Chauvin and subsequently El-Shamy depended on Galland's ghoul. Ultimately, Galland embellished the ghoul with a new feature that became a standard description of this creature in the West.

Finally, in an attempt to investigate the origins of Galland's idea of the ghoul that digs graves and eats corpses in Arabic sources, it is necessary to compare his description with some Arabic references to a certain animal that has similar characteristics. In old Arabic writings, the only account similar to Galland's ghoul is found in the popular description of the hyena. al-Dimiri (c. 1341–c. 1404) mentions that hyenas "are fond of digging graves due to their great appetite for eating human flesh"[26] (1978, vol. i, 641). Also, al-ʻAişami (?–c. 1699) cited anecdotal evidence of an event that occurred in Mecca in 1667, in which a hyena-like animal came close to an ass, so some men chased it. The animal ran to a nearby house and injured the woman living there. As a result, the men killed the animal and called it a "ghoul" because they did not know what it was (2007, vol. iii, 51). This tale suggests the proximity with which people viewed the two creatures. Furthermore, J.E. Hanauer documented several stories about the superstitious beliefs about animals among Jews, Christians, and Muslims during his journey to Palestine in the late nineteenth century. According to the Arab belief, if the hyena is "not content with digging up and devouring dead bodies," it would "often bewitch … the living and lure them to [its] den," and it is believed to appear to "the solitary wayfarer, rub against him endearingly and then run on ahead." According to Hanauer, this person becomes "instantly bewitched" and follows the hyena "as fast as he can 'til he gets into the beast's den and is devoured" (1907, 271). In folktales, Muhawi and Kanaana believe that the hyena is "traditionally linked with supernatural forces, its effect on human beings being considered similar to that of possession by the jinn" (1989, 43). Also, El-Shamy classifies motif (B14.5) "Ghoul (ogre) as hybrid of jinniyyah and hyena" (1995, 104) which corresponds with the possible claim cited above. As the hyena is well known to eat carcasses and produce some semi-human sounds such as crying and laughter, it can be easily confused with the ghoul. The abovementioned accounts are similar to the description of Galland's ghoul, signifying that he may have heard a similar account from an Arab friend, Ḥanna Dhiyab, who inspired the orphan tales in the *Arabian Nights*, or read somewhere about the belief in hyenas in the Arab world and applied such a description to the ghoul.

Nowadays, however, the ghoul has become part of Western culture and has featured in movies, fantasy prose and science fiction novels, children's cartoons, and video games. It is clear, however, that Galland was responsible for popularizing the *Arabian Nights* and consequently spreading the notion of the Westernized ghoul in the West. As a result of this, numerous literary works were written in English in which this monster played a role in the delineation of characters, or in the description of frightful locales, especially in gothic novels.

The ghoul in English literature

Many prominent English literary figures were fascinated with the notion of Galland's ghoul, because it offered extremely strange details about the exotic East that were useful for heightening the elements of fear and suspense in their works. According to different sources, the earliest reference to the ghoul in English literature was probably made in William Beckford's (1759–1844) *Vathek: An Arabian Tale* of 1786, which was translated from French into English by Beckford's friend, Samuel Henley. Since Vathek was originally written in French in 1782, Beckford used the French spelling and connotation of the word "goule" because he directly borrowed it from Galland's French translation of the *Arabian Nights* (Skeat 1910, 25; Kane 1933, 269).

Vathek is a Gothic novel that revolves around a real character called al-Wathiq bin Mu'tasim, the ninth Abbasid Caliph. The rest of the story is fictional and it deals with a man who manages to build a high tower from which he views all the states in the world, and later marries a very beautiful lady called Nouronihar, who also becomes involved in her husband's madness. Beckford used ghouls as malignant and fearful creatures in order to intensify the element of suspense and to give more scope for descriptions of a gothic nature. According to Beckford, Nouronihar, for instance, was once greatly frightened by "the stories of malignant Dives and dismal Goules [that] thronged into her memory," and the Caliph "looked not less pale and haggard than the goules that wander, at night, among the graves" (Beckford 1816, 145), and Bababalouk, who abducted Nouronihar's father to force her to marry the Caliph, asked the latter: "Ah, my lord! … do you then perform the office of a goul! Have you dug up the dead?" (Beckford 1816, 162). Along with adopting the spelling of "ghoul" introduced by Galland, Beckford's English editor cited Charles Richardson's (1775–1865) "Dissertation," prefixed to his *A New Dictionary of the English Language* (1836–7), to explain the term:

> "goule": Goules. Goul, or ghul in Arabic, signifies any terrifying object, which deprives people of the use of their senses. Hence it became the appellative of that species of monsters which was supposed to haunt forests, cemeteries, and other lonely places; and believed not only to tear in pieces the living, but to dig up and devour the dead.
>
> (Beckford 1816, 132)

As a matter of fact, Richardson, the etymologist, was harshly criticized by Daniel Webster (1782–1852) for his "ignorance of oriental languages," and because his "etymologies" were "frequently wrong" (Marchant 2004); thus, Richardson followed Galland's ghoul definition without altering it.

One of the horrific scenes in the novel is that which occurs when Carathis, the Caliph's mother and a renowned witch, takes some of her faithful followers with her to a cemetery. In an attempt to make a sacrifice, she tries to make a pact with the ghouls, saying: "So beautiful a cemetery must be haunted by gouls! … I will apply for directions to them; and, as an inducement, will invite them to regale on these fresh corpses" (Beckford 1816, 173–4). Carathis orders her black slaves, Nerkes and Cafour, to go and "knock against the sides of the tombs and strike up [the] delightful warblings," in order to awaken the ghouls. Beckford not only intensifies the horrific description of the ghouls but also that of the black slaves who are pictured as "full of joy" to see the ghouls.

Another notable example of the use of ghouls in romantic English literature is in the poem of "Lalla Rookh" (1817) by the Irish poet, singer, and songwriter Thomas Moore (1779–1852). Here, the Indian emperor, Aurungzebe, wanted his daughter, Lalla Rookh, to marry a prince called Aliris, son of King Abdalla of Bucharia. Aurungzebe thus sent a fancy caravan to Lalla Rookh in order to take her to Cashmere for the wedding. Along the road, she fell in love with a poet called Feramorz, and an inner conflict started between her mind and heart, but she discovered at the end that the poet was in fact Aliris himself. Moore included several stories in this long poem, such as "The Veiled Prophet of Khorassan," in which he described the agony of people being tormented by wars since the Caliph took up arms against "the false Prophet … / And of his host of infidels, who hurl'd / Defiance fierce at Islam and the world" (Moore 1890, 96). After describing a horrible scene involving dead and mutilated people, Zelica felt very afraid but everything "round seem'd tranquil even the foe had ceased / As if aware of that demoniac feast" (Moore 1890, 117). This demonic feast is reminiscent of ghouls devouring human flesh but figuratively applied by the poet to human beings killing each other in battle. In a further reference to ghouls, Moore mentions the following:

> But features horribler than hell e'er traced / On its own brood; no demon of the waste, / No churchyard ghole, caught lingering in the light / Of the bless'd sun, e'er blasted human sight.
>
> (Moore 1890, 118–19)

This demon is clearly the ghoul that is believed to live in the wilderness or wasteland. In order to explain the "Demon of the Waste," Moore cited a reference in a footnote from Mountstuart Elphinstone (1779–1859), a British diplomat, who, in 1815, wrote a book entitled *An Account of the Kingdom of Caubul and Its Dependencies*, in Persia, Tartary, and India:

> The Afghauns believe each of the numerous solitudes and deserts of their country to be inhabited by a lonely demon, whom they call The Ghoollee Beeabaun (the Goule or spirit of the waste). They represent him as a

> gigantic and frightful spectre, who devours any passenger whom chance may bring, within his haunts.
>
> (Elphinstone 1839, 291)

In another story within "Lallah Rookh" called "The Light of Haram," Moore mentioned Namouna, "the Enchantress," who protected herself from the evil magic of others and obtained many talismans, like the famous "gold gems of Afric" (1890, 278). Travelers used to wear them around their arms like the "wandering Arab," who wore it to "keep him from the Siltim's harm" (Moore 1890, 279). According to the poet's note citing Richard Richardson's "Dissertation," Siltim was a "demon, supposed to haunt woods, etc., in a human shape" (Moore 1980, 279). In fact, Siltim or Saltam in the Arabic language is "one of the names of the ghoul and is also applied to a tough person" (al-Iskafi 1998, 1050).

William Ernest Henley (1849–1903) is another well-known poet who tackled the image of the ghoul in his poem *Arabian Nights Entertainments* (Henley 1907, 57–75). This work starts with the story of a boy whose life was completely transformed because of a book called the *Arabian Nights*. When the poet hinted at the idea of going out at night, he referred to ghouls, and specifically to Amina, the enchantress in the "Story of Sidi Nouman":

> Haply a Ghoul
>
> Sat in the churchyard under a frightened moon, A thighbone in his fist, and glared
>
> At supper with a Lady: she who took
> Her rice with tweezers grain by grain.
>
> (Henley 1907, ll. 296–300, 71)

It seems that Amina has fascinated many writers of English literature due to her unprecedented evil character, as she represented an oriental femme fatale. Charles Dickens (1812–70), probably more than any other English writer, used the ghoul in his novels as an inspiration for a number of ugly, fearful, and sometimes fierce persons. In "A Christmas Tree" of 1850, Dickens takes the reader into different fairy worlds including "the bright *Arabian Nights*" (Dickens 1913, 7). From the few details given, Dickens recalled the "Story of Sidi Nouman," which included the metamorphosed husband "who jumped upon the baker's counter and put his paw on the piece of bad money" (1913, 8). The evil woman, Amina, was mentioned as "the awful lady, who was a ghoule, [and who] could only peck [the rice] by grains, because of her nightly feasts in the burial-place" (Dickens 1913, 8). Similarly, in her novel *Cranford* of 1853, Elizabeth Gaskell (1810–65) introduced Miss Matty, who was depicted just like Amina. Matty "picked up her peas, one by one, on the point of the prongs, much as Amine ate her grains of rice after her previous feast with the Ghoul" (Gaskell 1914, 53).

The Brontë sisters were also influenced by the concept of the ghoul as presented in the *Arabian Nights*. Emily Brontë (1818–48) implied in *Wuthering Heights* of 1847 that Heathcliff might be a ghoul by stating that he went "to bed, and … wanted nothing to eat till morning" (1847b, 397). Just as Amina left her husband at night heading toward the cemetery, Heathcliff used to leave the house at night:

> We heard him mount the stairs directly; he did not proceed to his ordinary chamber, but turned into that with the panelled bed—its window, as I mentioned before, is wide enough for anybody to get through, and it struck me, that he plotted another midnight excursion, which he had rather we had no suspicion of.
>
> (Brontë 1847b, 397)

Thus, Ellen Dean, the housekeeper, wonders "Is he a ghoul or a vampire?," referring to the fact that she had "read of such hideous incarnate demons" (Brontë 1847, 397). In the same context, Mr. Rochester in Charlotte Brontë's (1816–55) *Jane Eyre* of 1847 asks Jane to dine with him, but she hesitates for a while, and he thus starts wondering: "Do you suppose I eat like an ogre or a ghoul, that you dread being the companion of my repast?" (Brontë 1847, 244).

In short, many English writers were influenced by Galland's ghoul and its accompanying enchantress, Amina, and used them in their works without any notable altering of their features. Most writers stress that the ghoul digs graves and eats human corpses – which is completely at odds with the old Arabic notion of this monster – and which seems to be a direct result of Galland's translation of the *Arabian Nights*. More than 2,000 years have passed since the ghoul was first envisioned by a few Arab Bedouins in the heartland of Arabia, but it has refused to fade away from people's memories. It eventually crossed the desert border to enter Asia and Africa, but it was Antoine Galland who made the ghoul travel further to reach Europe after giving it its new form.

In addition to the classical description of the ghoul in Arabic culture, there is another type of ghoul-like creature called Shiqq. I will present below an analytical discussion of this devilish beast because of its importance and relevance in understanding the "other side" of the ghoul.

The Shiqq and ghoul

Several Arabic sources referred to the Shiqq or nasnas meaning "half" and "only one half is visible" (Marzolph and Leeuwen 2004, 535). In folktales, the "person with half a body" and the "one-sided man" are well-known motifs (F525) and (F525.1) (Thompson 2002; El-Shamy 2004, 163). In pre-Islamic Arabic accounts, there was the famous story of "Allqumah Bin Safwan Bin

Umayah al-Kinani" who once rode a donkey and went on a clear night to Mecca. He reached a place called Yaḥuman[27] where he met the Shiqq carrying a sword; however, they both fell dead at the end of the fight (al-Qazwini 1980, 237; al-Dimiri 1978, 601–2; al-Jahidh 1969, 206–7; Al-Zamakhshari 1992, 379–80).

After Islam, the Shiqq remained alive in the minds of the people who believed in its existence. For instance, al-Jahidh said that this creature was known to be "a kind of genie appearing to travelers to kill them either by frightening them or by beating them" (1969, 206). This is similar to the accounts above of the ghoul. However, the shape of the Shiqq was peculiar because it had only "one eye, one hand, and one leg." al-Qazwini further clarified that the Shiqq was "a devilish creature which looked like a half human" (1980, 237). In the *Arabian Nights*, "The Story of the Sage and the Scholar" referred to nasnas, denoting that this was a common belief held by Arab people. In spite of the pre-Islamic origins of Shiqq, Arab Bedouins held this creature as part of their popular beliefs for many centuries since Charles Montagu Doughty (1843–1926) referred in *Travels in Arabia Deserta* (1888) to it. Doughty's traveling desert companion mentioned that there was a genie type with "horrible" looks; "certain of them have but one eye in the midst of their faces" (1964, 17). Doughty met an Arab Bedouin who swore that he saw a "ghrôl" or "ghrûl" in the desert and provided the following description:

> [It had] a cyclops' eye set in the midst of her human-like head, long beak of jaws, in the ends one or two great sharp tusks, long neck; her arms like chicken's fledgling wings, the fingers of her hands not divided; the body big as a camel's, but in shape as the ostrich;[28] the sex is only feminine, she has a foot as the ass' hoof, and a foot as an ostrich. She entices passengers, calling to them over the waste by their names, so that they think it is their own mother's or their sister's voice.
>
> (1933, 53)

As can be seen in the account above, there seems to be some overlap between the ghoul and Shiqq, and Doughty considered these tales ridiculous, saying that "no man, but Philemon, lived a day fewer for laughing" (1933, 53) at such stories. Nevertheless, Hasan El-Shamy classified tens of Arab folktales that belong to 327B (The Dwarf and the Giant) in which Nuṣṣ-nuṣaiṣ (Half) and Ḥdaydun were the main characters (2004, 1001). Also, motif (G415.1) "Ogress poses as man's sister and invites him to live in her house" (El-Shamy 2004, 1073) is similar to the account mentioned above. Again, the legend of the half person has not faded away in the popular imagination, though the one mentioned in folktales is rather friendly and carries human features, unlike the devilish Shiqq or nasnas.[29] In the following section, there is a discussion of Charles Perrault's *Le Petit Poucet* folktale, and its possible Arabic source, taking the ghoul figure and Galland's possible influence as a central discussion point.

Charles Perrault's *Le Petit Poucet*

As mentioned above, the ghoul is a well-known monster, described in old Arabic lexicons as a devilish genie that preys on humans in the wilderness and deserted valleys,[30] and sometimes takes its victims to its dwelling. This description is also found in Arabic folktales and some *Arabian Nights* tales,[31] where the motif of people being lured to a ghoul's dwelling or children wandering into an ogre's house is common.

For instance, "Fatma the Lovely," a compilation of Arabic folktales by Ahmed Shahi and F.C.T. Moore (1978), contained a Nubian tale. The seven girls who ventured into the bush to fetch wood are important to the story's premise. They were drawn to the distant fire and tempted to approach it, but an ogress was waiting for them. As the ogress revealed that she intended to consume the seven children, Fatma made the decision to trick the creature in order to escape with the other women. In the end, Fatma was successful in escaping, and the ogress was put to death (125–6). Christine Goldberg used the Middle Eastern tale "Halfling," about a child named Mqidech who had seven brothers, as a source for her research. Mqidech is the youngest among his brothers and his name denotes "half-man" (344). The ogre takes them captive and they manage to escape with the help of Mqidech. Finally, El-Shamy refers to tens of other Arabic stories that have similar tale types such as "Nus Nusais and Hdaydun (Halved person)" (tale type 327B), "Thumbling as Rescuer," who saves his siblings from the ogress, and "Tom Thumb" (0700) whose story deals with the adventures of a boy the size of a finger joint (El-Shamy 1001 & 1008).

Other tales dealing with the ghoul as a fearful human-eating monster that could smell humans in its house are found in Arabic folktales. Ibrahim Muhawi and Sharif Kanaana (1989) referred to two similar tales in their study of Palestinian folktales. The first, entitled "The Brave Lad" (148–50), is narrated by a 95-year-old woman from the village of Rammun in Ramallah and deals with a young man who decided to enter the ghoul's cave in the forest in order to kill it because its crimes terrified the people. Surprised, the man found the ghoul's beautiful wife whom the ghoul had taken captive. She hated the ghoul and wanted to escape, but could not find a way. As they were about to leave the cave, the ghoul arrived, so the lady hid the man in the wardrobe. The ghoul was furious because it smelled human flesh, but could not find any stranger inside its dwelling. With the help of the young man, the lady managed to kill the ghoul, take its treasure, and save the town.

In addition, ghouls having seven heads are known in Arabic folktales (G361.1.4) (El-Shamy, 125), especially in North Africa, and this physical feature adds to their horrific description and increases fear. The English traveler,

Edward Westermarck (1899), confirmed the belief in seven-headed monsters when he visited the Arabs of Morocco in the nineteenth century. They thought of the genies as having

> no fixed forms, but may assume almost any shape they like. They appear now as men, and now as goats, cats, dogs, donkeys, tortoises, snakes, or other animals, now as monsters with the body of a man and the legs of a donkey, now in other shapes, sometimes, for instance, with seven heads. (253)

The belief that ghouls only die by striking them once is a pre-Islamic belief that is cited above. Perrault could have used the tale above and added other features from his own, for in the first part of the seventeenth century, it was common in France to join two tales together as in Madame d'Aulnoy's "Pinette Cendron" which contained the plots of Perrault's *Le Petit Poucet* and "Cendrillon" (Trinquet 2007, 34).

Critics have been analyzing Charles Perrault's *Histoires ou contes du temps passe, avec des moralites: Contes de ma mere l'Oye* since its publication in 1697. One of Perrault's tales, *Le Petit Poucet* or "Little Thumbling" (ATU tale type 327) (Perrault, 29–44), has received a lot of attention from critics who have different views about its origin. Although many stories from different European nations and from India have been suggested as sources, they often lack satisfactory evidence due to different details presented (Lang 1888, civ–cxv; Deulin 1878, 325–67; Cosquin 1922, 349–99; Saintyves 1923, 233–349). Some critics have even suggested that *Le Petit Poucet* imitated Homer's *Odysseus* in his plight, while others believed that Perrault invented the story himself and it was not based on any pre-existing tale. Instead, he "first invented stories before they were disseminated among the people," according to Wilhelm Grimm's introduction to the 1812 edition of *Kinder und Hausmarchen* (see also Tatar 2003, 257).

There have been few studies exploring the possibility that an Arabic folktale may have influenced *Le Petit Poucet*, despite some critics believing that it served as inspiration for later works like "Pinette Cendron" by Madame d'Aulnoy and "Hansel and Gretel" by the Brothers Grimm (Opie 1992, 34 & 236; Murphy 2000, 47). I argue that the first part of *Le Petit Poucet* could have been derived from an old Arabic folktale. Perrault may have learned about this tale through the Catalan oral tradition or his friend, Antoine Galland. Furthermore, I suggest that Perrault likely borrowed from other sources rather than inventing the entire story and characters, as some critics have claimed. By analyzing the cultural interaction and transmission of folktales between the East and West, I aim to demonstrate the universality of the theme and tale type found in *Le Petit Poucet*.

For example, Abdul Karim Al-Juhayman collected the Arabic folktale in the late 1970s in the Arabian Peninsula as part of his influential work, *Popular*

Myths from the Heartland of Arabia (vol. IV, 55–68). Al-Juhayman made it clear that he recorded the tales exactly as he heard them, without embellishing or adding any further details (Vol. I, 12). The tale was obtained directly from the accounts of Bedouins, but it has not been analyzed in-depth until now. Hasan El-Shamy's extensive work on folktales from the Arab world referenced it once as matching the tale type of "the children and the ogre" (based on Aarne and Thompson's scheme, 1964, tale type 327), including the sub-type of "ogre's wife (daughter) protects his victims-to-be" (tale type 327D, 164). However, I contend that this Arabic folktale, known as "Safir's Tale," also contains elements of sub-type tale type 327A, "the parents abandon their children in the forest," and sub-type tale type 327B, "the dwarf and the giant" (Aarne & Thompson, 116). In summary, the plot of "Safir's Tale" revolves around the abandonment of children in the forest by their parents and their subsequent encounter with an ogre and his family. In the following section, we will consider the lexical evidence in order to investigate the possible link between Perrault's *Le Petit Poucet* and Arabic oral tradition.

Philological connections

In order to understand the possible circumstances that led to the writing of *Le Petit Poucet*, one has to examine the period during which our French author lived. The French interest in the literature and culture of what was then considered "the Orient" was as old as the Crusades themselves, but their preoccupation increased greatly during the reign of King Louis XIV (c. 1661–90), a leader who encouraged the study of languages and cultures of other parts of the world. This interest was reflected in the increasing number of travelers to the East, the trade with the Ottoman Empire, and a Christian religious zeal to convert Muslims.[32] French writers of fairy tales emerged during this period because they were supported by patrons and had suitable literary backgrounds. Writers like Madame L'Héritier, Madame d'Aulnoy, Madame de Murat, and Mlle de la Force "composed lengthy tales about fairies" (Bottigheimer 2004, 261). As for Charles Perrault, he was, in fact, the pioneer in popularizing the fairy tale not only in France, but also in Europe. He was considered "the first man in France" to write fairy tales and "certainly the first Academician" (Warner 1990, 10).

Perrault was supported by Jean-Baptiste Colbert (1619–83), who was responsible for the royal patronage of learning and served as finance minister to King Louis XIV. When Colbert heard about Perrault's skills, he hired him as First Secretary in the Department of Buildings and promoted him afterward to Controleur General de la Surintendance des Batiments (Carpenter & Prichard 1991, 402). Perrault started interacting with French intellectuals and became the center of attention due to his career and literary reputation.

Among Perrault's most distinguished friends was Barthelemy d'Herbelot de Molainville (1625–95) whose patron happened to be Colbert as well.

D'Herbelot was a French scholar who traveled several times to Italy to collect Arabic, Turkish, and Persian manuscripts which resulted in his substantial work *Bibliotheque orientale* (1697), which is mentioned above. He also used to interact with travelers coming to the Italian seaports from different Eastern countries in order to become familiar with their languages and cultures. Antoine Galland, who himself was a close friend of Perrault, worked with d'Herbelot as his assistant in writing the *Bibliotheque*, which is considered the first encyclopedia on Islam written in a European language, as mentioned above.

Bibliotheque orientale, which was published in the same year as Perrault's *The Tales of Mother Goose*, is considered one of the most influential works on Islam and the Arab world in Europe. In fact, "many readers valued d'Herbelot and Galland's book as a source of Oriental tales" (Dew 2004, 234), and several French and British writers drew information from it when they tackled the subject of Islam or Arabs. For instance, William Beckford used the *Bibliotheque* in his novel *Vathek: An Arabian Tale* (1786), and Robert Southey's "Thalaba" was directly influenced by the same work (Irwin, 15). Some scholars now believe that *Bibliotheque orientale* even contains parallel stories to some *Arabian Nights* tales such as the story of "Buhlul the Jester" (Marzolph & van Leeuwen 2004, Vol. I, 129).

Most importantly, Perrault expressed in *Les hommes illustres qui ont paru en France pendant le XVII siècle* his indebtedness to the Bibliotheque that it contained "the complete history of an undiscovered planet, adorned with its architecture, quarrels, the terror of its mythologies, and the mumble of its languages." Furthermore, Perrault felt that the *Bibliotheque* showed "new historical stories, new political realities, new morals, new poetry; in other words, a new sky, a new earth" (2002, 427). For the first time in Europe, the ghoul was presented in the *Bibliotheque*; "Gaul" and "Afriet" were described as Islamic myths suggesting the most fearful kind of "Ginns" (2001, Vol. 5, 193). These new creatures were definitely a source of inspiration for many writers; in fact, it was not a coincidence that Perrault became the first person to introduce Europeans to the words "ogre" and "ogress" in *Histoires ou contes du temps passe, avec des moralites: Contes de ma mere l'Oye*, two terms whose etymology remained "uncertain and disputed" (Rose 2001, 274; *Oxford English Dictionary*, 2004 & 2008 eds.). Indeed, Perrault used the word "ogre" to mean "ghoul," and a few years later, when Antoine Galland translated the *Arabian Nights*, he followed Perrault's device and changed the use of "ghoul" into "ogre," as stated above. In "The Story of the Vizier That Was Punished" (n.d., 77–79), Galland referred to an "ogre" instead of a "ghoul," saying, "The Lady was a Hogres, wife to one of those Savage Demons, called Hogres, who stay in remote places, and make use of a thousand wiles to surprise and devour passengers" (n.d., 78). Later on, Western writers started using the word "ogre" to refer to a man-eating monster as a result of Galland's popular translation of the *Arabian Nights*.

In the "Preface" to his selection of the *Arabian Nights* (1929), Andrew Lang mentioned that the work attracted many Europeans because they "were delighted with Ghouls (who lived among the tombs) and Geni, who seemed to be a kind of ogre" (1929, ix). As further evidence that the two words were related, the word "ogre" was usually called "Le Sarrasin" in popular French versions of fairy tales up to the late nineteenth century in order to refer to the qualities of "ferocity and stupidity" (Lang, xli). In fact, the negative association between the ogre and the "Saracen" or Muslim is rooted in the nature of the historical relationship between Europe and Islam, but it clearly reflects the origin of the word "ogre." There was a pattern in medieval Europe that linked the Saracen's figure with the devil or ugly monsters (Al-Jubouri 1972, 58). Even the Prophet Muhammad's name referred to a "demon" in the Middle Ages (Smith 1977, 3) as the different derivations of his name had other connotations; for instance, "Mahound" meant a "monster" and a "hideous creature" in the sixteenth century, "Mahomet" denoted an "idol" in the seventeenth century, and the word "Turk" meant a "hideous image to frighten children" that lasted many centuries (*Oxford English Dictionary*, 1989 and 2000).

Possible means of oral tradition transmission

How did Perrault and his contemporaries come to know about Arabic folktales? In 1819, Wilhelm Grimm pointed out in *Kinder und Hausmiirchen* that many folktales from different cultures may look similar due to a mere "accident"; however, he stressed that some stories were so similar that they "quite preclude … all acceptation of the idea of a merely apparent relationship" (1884, 575). In other words, the similarity that one finds in the motifs, tale type, and nature of characters in folktales coming from far away is due to the oral tradition that plays a major role in the spread of ideas, stories, and beliefs. Andrew Lang elaborates on the illogicality of searching for a folktale source in the same place where it is circulated:

> But it is impossible to argue that the birthplace of a tale is the country where it is first found in a literary shape. The stories must have been current in the popular mouth long before they won their way into written literature, on tablets of clay or on papyrus.
>
> (cxiv)

There are two possible ways by which Perrault came to know about "Safir's Tale." First, the tale could have been passed on to Perrault through the Catalan oral tradition. As a matter of fact, tale types 327A and 327B are well known in Catalan folktales (Aarne & Thompson 1964, 117–18). According to Perrault's young niece, Marie Jeanne L'Héritier de Villandon, who also wrote fairy tales, the origins of European fairytales went back to the "Gallic matrix" of the Middle Ages, popular "among the troubadours and storytellers of Provence" (Warner 1990, 7). In fact, the root of the word "troubadour" itself is Arabic based on "tarab" which means to "entertain by singing." The Arabic influence on troubadours' poetry is referred to by many scholars ranging from citing the practice of borrowing rhyme schemes from Arabic poetry to using the courtly love tradition (Sutherland 1956, 199–215; Gorton 1974, 11–16). Menocal 1987 asserts that "the birth of Provencal troubadour poetry occurred at a time and place when the Arabic world and its culture were of immediate fascination and importance" (31). To take an example from folktales, the Belgian critic, Charles Deulin, found a Catalonian tale entitled "Lo Noy Petit, Le Petit Gars" in "The Catalan lo Rondallayre" in which three brothers were abandoned by their parents, and the youngest thought of finding a way back home by using white pebbles and then crumbs. This story seems to be closely linked to the Arabic version of *Le Petit Poucet* cited here (341–2).[33] In fact, the literature of Catalonia was mainly based on troubadours' literary experience, and the inhabitants of the country were greatly influenced by the Arabs and their culture because of the several centuries of Arab rule over Spain. When Perrault started writing his fairy tales, Catalonia was already under French rule (between 1694 and 1697), and many people there spoke French. Furthermore, Robert Irwin 2004 stated that the tales of "the Orient" were well known in medieval Italy and were circulated in southern Italy and Spain as part of the folk tradition (96–100 and 63–102). However, they were usually "stripped of their specifically Islamic and Oriental features" (101). In this respect, Sir Walter Scott 1802 commented:

> Intercourse of France and Italy with the moors of Spain, and the prevalence of the Arabic, as the language of science in the dark ages, facilitated the introduction of their mythology amongst the nations of the west. Hence, the romances of France, of Spain, and of Italy, unite in describing the Fairy as an inferior spirit, in a beautiful female form, possessing many of the amiable qualities of the eastern Peri. Nay, it seems sufficiently clear, that the romancers borrowed from the Arabs, not merely the general idea concerning those spirits, but even the names of individuals amongst them. (176)

Finally, the argument that Perrault's *Le Petit Poucet* is partly taken from the Italian folk narrative of Giambattista Basile's "Ninillo and Nennella" in the Pentamerone (Day 5, tale 8) (Deulin 1878, 332; Carpenter & Prichard 1991, 260; Lang 1888, cvi) appears rather weak if one examines the different details in the two stories. However, it remains probable that Basile "gathered stories circulating in the oral tradition in his time. Some of these tales might already have contained motifs and images of Oriental origin" (Marzolph and van Leeuwen 2004 Vol. II, 491). In other words, Perrault was indirectly influenced by this folk tradition by his presumed borrowing from Basile. Indeed, the evidence suggests that Perrault was mostly influenced by the Catalan oral tradition that was directly influenced by the Arabs.

The other possible way by which Perrault heard about this story comes through his friend, Antoine Galland, the first translator of the *Arabian Nights* into a European language. Here, it is important to turn to the way the *Arabian Nights* had been translated and rewritten by Galland between 1704 and 1717. Many critics believe that some tales in the *Arabian Nights* were taken directly from the Arab oral tradition. Due to the encouragement of learning languages and cultures, an influx of Arab Christian monks in France discussed religious matters and shared popular stories from Arab culture. The French interest in this area came with the colonial expansion of France into the "Eastern Mediterranean from the end of the seventeenth century on" (Said 2003, 17). In 1692, the French Jesuits requested approval to welcome "foreign students from the Orient with the idea that these students, once converted to the Catholic faith, should return to their home countries to help the Jesuits introduce it to the native populace" (Kimpton 2006, 74).[34] French scholars like Galland made good use of having Arabic speakers in Paris. In 1709, Galland met a Maronite Syrian called Hannā Diyāb, who helped him compose what are now called the "orphan tales" such as "Ali Baba and the Forty Thieves," "Aladdin," and "The Story of Sidi Nauman," the collection of which does not bear any resemblance to other versions of the *Arabian Nights* (Marzolph & van Leeuwen 2004, Vol. 2, 582–3; Mahdi 1995, 32; Haddawy 1992, xvii; Larzul 2004, 258). The trend of bringing Arab scholars to France in order to assist in the translation and even in the writing of works continued for more than a century as seen in the cases of Michel Sabbagh and Mordecai ibn al-Najjar (Marzolph 2004, Vol. 2, 695).

In addition, borrowing from other writers without referring to sources was customary in France because writing and publishing works was the primary goal as was the case with Madame d'Aulnoy's "Pinette Cendron." Furthermore, Soriano 1968 confirms that Perrault could have borrowed some of his tales from the Middle East through his friends François Bernier or Antoine Galland who both journeyed to the East and had plenty of knowledge about its customs and traditions (152). In fact, Perrault personally corresponded with Bernier in 1672 (275). It appears that Perrault must have heard some of the Arabic stories mentioned above but later changed some details and altered names to make them suitable for his French audience.

In considering the origin of Perrault's other tales, Andrew Lang and Charles Deulin believe that an old Arab (Swahili) tale closely resembles Perrault's "Puss in Boots," with the only difference being the presence of a gazelle instead of a cat that helps the poor man achieve his dreams (Lang 1888, lxxix–lxxxii; Deulin 1878, 204). Lang comments, "From Arabia the tale has been carried into Russia, Scandinavia, Italy, India, and France, often leaving its moral behind it, and always exchanging its gazelle for some other beast-hero" (lxxxii). In fact, Perrault was used to changing details and deviating from the original oral tales. For instance, the addition of the "little red cap" in "Little

Red Riding Hood" was meant to "indicate the social status of the young girl and is not found in any of the oral variants other than those directly influenced by Perrault" (Clements 2006, Vol. II, 266). Also, the French critic Marc Soriano 1968 stated that Perrault's *Les Souhaits ridicules* ("The Ludicrous Wishes") has possible Persian, Hebrew, Arabic, or Greek sources because there are no obvious traces of its European origin (109). Finally, tale type 327D ("Ogre's wife (daughter) protects his victims-to-be") was known in Zanzibar (Aarne & Thompson 1964, 118), a place that was controlled for a long time by the Arabs.

It seems apparent that Charles Perrault was influenced by Arabic folktales, whether directly or indirectly. He is naturally associated with French tales for children, but clearly, there are varying influences on his stories well beyond French borders. Obviously, the oral tradition played a major role in the dissemination of tales from Arabia to Europe via various means. Indeed, *Le Petit Poucet* has roots in several different cultures, and its small hero figure enjoys wide popularity around the globe despite the different names he has taken.

To sum up, the ghoul is very popular in the oral tales of Arab Bedouins. As proof, Western travelers who visited the Arab region in the eighteenth and nineteenth centuries referred to this monster mainly when they encountered the Bedouins. However, when Antoine Galland translated the *Arabian Nights* in the eighteenth century, he transformed the monster into a vampire-like creature and he influenced numerous literary figures possibly including his friend, Charles Perrault.

Notes

1 The content of this chapter has previously appeared as research papers published in the following journals: Al-Rawi, A. K. (2009). The Arabic ghoul and its Western transformation. *Folklore*, 120(3), 291–306. Al-Rawi, A. (2009). The mythical ghoul in Arabic culture. *Cultural Analysis*, 8, 45–69. Al-Rawi, A. K. (2010). Charles Perrault's "Le Petit Poucet" and its possible Arabic Influences. *Bookbird*, 48(1), 31.

2 There are plenty of Arabic words whose origins are derived from the old languages of Mesopotamia. For instance, the Arabic word "harem" that is associated with women, stems from the Akkadian word "Harimtu" which means "sacred prostitute dedicated to the godhead." The ending "u" is usual in such an old language and was omitted in Arabic. As for ghoul, the Arabic root of the word is "ghâl" which means "kill"; hence, the Akkadian word "Gallu" explains the etymological connection.

3 According to Ibn Durayd (838–933), the Qutrub is the male ghoul (1987, 1121).

4 The Marid is a type of a devil whose name means "rebel" because it has rebelled against God (al-Zubaydi 1998, 165).

5 For the detailed meaning of "hamah", see note (11).

6 The Quran contains a verse that describes the devils eavesdropping on Heaven in order to overhear God's angels; thus, meteors are thrown at them (al-Safat (7–10) 446).

7 The most famous story was that of the Arab poet Thabit Bin Jabir Bin Sufyan or Ta'abbatah Sharran who saw a ghoul in the shape of a ram (al-Isfahani 1983, 144). For more details, see Ahmed K. Al-Rawi's "The Arabic Ghoul and Its Western Transformation", *Folklore*, Vol. 120, Issue 3 (December 2009): 291–306.

8 The two words are used interchangeably to refer to the same creature; however, the si'lwah or si'lah is always feminine.
9 The Western beliefs in the spirits of the wilderness, Joan the Wad, Jack-o'-lantern, and will-o'-the-wisp are similar to the description of this ghoul.
10 'adwa or "infection" here means transmission of diseases. Before Islam, Arabs thought that the mythical animal şifr could be transmitted like a disease from one person to another (al-Nawawi 1971, vol. xiv, 215; 'Abdulwahab n.d., 373). The other interpretation, according to al-Nawawī, was that the Prophet stressed that diseases could not be transmitted to other people without God's will (1971, vol. vi, 325).
11 Arabs before Islam used to believe in taṭayur or "portents". If any traveler attempts to leave somewhere, he/she has to check the signs by letting a bird fly before the journey takes place. If it goes to the right side, it is a good herald, whereas the left side is a bad omen, so the traveler must postpone the whole trip.
12 Before Islam, Arabs believed that the predatory bird hamah or the owl was a very bad omen. If such a bird dies near someone's house, the house's owner should expect that one of the residents will die. In addition, Arabs believed that the bones of the deceased or their souls would later turn into predatory birds as one way of incarnation; as a result, the Prophet emphasized the falsity of the mythical basis of such a belief (al-Nawawi 1971, vol. xiv, 215; al-Maliki 1994, 342; 'Abdulwahab n.d., 378; al-Dimiri 1978, vol. i, 226). To this day, the owl is viewed as a bad omen by many Arabs. In addition, the hamah was believed to be a worm leaving a man's skull if he was killed without being avenged. It would circle around the man's tomb saying: "water me," asking for vengeance. Jews in Arabia used to think that the hamah would circle round a man's tomb for seven days before departing ('Abdulwahab n.d., 379). Hasan El-Shamy assigns for the hamah motif (E0451.9.1) "hamah ceases to appear when revenge is accomplished" and motif (E0473.2) "ghost of murdered person in owl-form that cries for revenge" (2008, 114), but he classifies the hamah as part of the "Soul" or "Self" section instead of being a subheading of "Zoological Supernatural Beings" since the hamah was believed to be an animal-like creature.
13 Banu meant pain in the stomach that could infect other people (al-Tamimi 1967, 199; al-Sajistani n.d., 520), and sometimes it would infect livestock cattle ('Abdulwahab n.d., 379). Furthermore, it was believed to be the other name of şifr, which was one of the months in the Islamic calendar. Though Arabs believed that there were sacred months during which fighting was prohibited, some used to change the rules of war each year. They would sanction the war once but might allow it the next year according to their interests. The Prophet banned this practice (al-Tamimi, 197–8). In addition, al-Sajistani mentioned a third explanation of the word "banu" saying that Arabs used to regard şifr as an ill-omened month and the Prophet corrected that view (n.d., 18).
14 Abu Sadat al-Jazri (c. 1149–c. 1209) mentioned that şifr was a kind of serpent that inhabited the stomach and used to sting a man when he felt hungry (1979, 35). In this way, Arabs explained hunger pangs as şifr stinging them. In folktales, El-Shamy classifies a similar motif (G328.1) as a "serpent inside man's body eats all his food" (1995, 148). In fact, sifr can be simply a tapeworm, a kind of helminthiasis, that usually infects, due to contaminated water or food, the digestive tracts of human beings, wherein it grows rapidly and reaches sometimes several meters in size.
15 Naw' was the old belief that meteors or "falling stars" would certainly bring rain. The Prophet emphasized that the falling stars had no effect, but it was God's will that could bring rain and generate the wind (al-Tabari 1984, 208).
16 Other Muslim scholars believed that Muhammed did not negate the existence of ghouls; instead, he only said that they had no power to change their shapes (al-Kufi

1988, 311; al-Nawawi 1971, vol. xiv, 217; al-Siuti 1996, 239; al-'Asqalanī 1959, 159; al-'Abbadi 1994, 292). al-Burrusi (?–c. 1918) elaborated by saying that ghouls could not delude people or change their visages, but the enchantresses of genies, the si'lwah, could if it encountered genies (1911, vol. iv, 450).

17 Westermarck also noticed that Arabs in Morocco believed that genies have "no fixed forms, but may assume almost any shape they like. They appear now as men, and now as goats, cats, dogs, donkeys, tortoises, snakes, or other animals, now as monsters with the body of a man and the legs of a donkey, now in other shapes, sometimes, for instance, with seven heads" (1899, 253).

18 al-Qazwini gives the same description but calls this devilish creature "Ghaddar" ("perfidious") (1980, 237), and Robert Irwin calls this kind of creature a "homosexual ghoul" (2004, 206).

19 In *Myths of Babylonia and Assyria*, Donald A. Mackenzie described the widespread belief in Babylonia that some sick people were thought to be possessed by a devilish creature. "It had therefore to be expelled by performing a magical ceremony and repeating a magical formula. The demon was either driven or enticed away" (1910, 234).

20 According to the *Al-Mawrid Dictionary: Arabic/English*, the word "si'alwah" is translated from Arabic into English as "ogress," because the latter has no equivalence in Arabic (al-Ba'labaki 2006, 630); therefore, ogre and ghoul are used interchangeably by some writers. Also, the word "huqur" in the Arabic language is close to "ogre," standing for a fearful and stupid "giant who is very tall" (Ibn Mandhur 2005, 4143).

21 The term "Sidi," which means "my master" or "Sir," is used exclusively by Arabs residing in North Africa, particularly in Morocco and Algeria, to show respect. Hence, this story was clearly written in one of the Arab countries in North Africa.

22 Other additions to the ghoul's description include Anthony S. Mercatante's reversal of Galland's account: "Ghouls eat corpses of young children, often taking bodies from graves. If no graveyard is available, they will pursue live victims" (Mercatante 1988, 275). Other mistakes are also made by some writers such as Ulrich Marzolph & van Leeuwen, who mentions in *The Arabian Nights Encyclopedia* that ghouls are giant creatures: "The ghoul is a giant cannibal jinnî" (2004, vol. 2, 535). In fact, this "giant" creature referred to by Marzolph resembles the European ogre rather than the Arabic ghoul.

23 As far as I am aware, there appears to be only one – possibly doubtful – reference to male ghouls residing in graveyards and devouring corpses. This occurs in Hasan M. El-Shamy's major work on the classification of international folktales in the Arab world. El-Shamy includes motif G20.0.2§ (Necrophagus Persons: eaters of dead bodies), in the "motif-spectrum" of tale-type 366A§, Cadaver (Corpse) Reclaims its Canabalized Organs from A Ghoul (Necrophagous Persons), in this work. However, it is not clear from the work whether the tale refers to male or female necrophagous persons. Furthermore, the tale was documented by El-Shamy in Brooklyn, New York, in June 1961, rather than in the Arab world (El-Shamy 2004, 183). As full source details and the content of the tale itself do not appear to be available at this point, the import of the reference must remain unclear until further research on the matter can be carried out.

24 "Ghoul, or goul: these are, according to the Mohammedan religion, spirits devouring the corpses in cemeteries."

25 Lane referred in *Manners and Customs of the Modern Egyptians and Arabian Society in the Middle Ages* to the Arabs' superstitious belief in "Ghools," "Seạláh," or "Saạláh" and said that there was no foundation for their belief. In a chapter called "Demonology" in *Arabian Society*, Lane said at the end: "I must beg the reader to remark that the superstitious fancies which it describes are prevalent among all classes of the Arabs, and the Muslims in general, learned as well as vulgar" (1987,

46). Lane's observation could be partly right because he wrote his works at a time when the majority of the people were uneducated, and the Bedouins' tribal customs and beliefs were widely spread in the society due to many centuries of regression.

26 al-Dimiri further says that Arabs make comparisons between humans and hyenas to refer to "an ugly looking woman from debased origins or an old witch" (1978, 644).

27 al-Jahidh said that the place was called azman wall instead of Yahuman.

28 al-Qazwini referred to another devilish creature called Dilhab that appeared in the shape of a human riding on an ostrich. It lived on sea islands and ate outcasts who were driven by the sea after being shipwrecked. Also, it was reputed to have a shrill cry that would make any person faint upon hearing it (1980, 237).

29 Surprisingly, the Swiss psychologist Carl G. Jung (1875–1961) reported during the summer of 1920 that while he was staying in an old farmhouse in Buckinghamshire he saw a weird creature appearing, specifically at night. Aside from the other descriptions given, Jung stated: "[I] opened my eyes. There, beside me on the pillow, I saw the head of an old woman, and the right eye, wide open, glared at me. The left half of the face was missing below the eye. The sight of it was so sudden and unexpected that I leapt out of bed with one bound, lit the candle, and spent the rest of the night in an armchair" (1977, 323–4). Similar to al-Jahidh and Burton's explanations of the ghoul's existence, Jung interpreted this apparition as a hallucinatory experience due to exhaustion, fear, and recalling memories of a particular lady. Jung commented on the sounds he heard in the room saying that they were "probably not objective noises, but noises in the ear which seemed to me occurring objectively in the room. In my peculiar hypnoid state, they appeared exaggeratedly loud … My torpor was associated with an inner excitation probably corresponding to fear" (1977, 325).

30 In Arabic mythology, valleys were mostly associated with genies. The Arabic word "'U'bqqar," which means "genius," was derived from a valley's name because it was believed that people could go mad if they went there due to the presence of genies.

31 See, for instance, the "Story of Fourth Voyage of the Es-Sindibad of the Sea" (Lane 1865, 35–49; Burton 1886–8, Vol. VI, 34–48) and "The Tale of the King's Son and the She-Ghoul" in the Arabic version of the *Arabian Nights* (1992, 42–55).

32 For a detailed study of the French interest in the East at that period, see Nicholas Dew, *The Pursuit of Oriental Learning in Louis XIV's France*, unpublished PhD thesis, Oxford University, 1999. See especially chapters 1 and 4 which concentrate on Barthelemy d'Herbelot's *Bibliotheque orientale*. See also Ina Baghdiantz McCabe's *Orientalism in Early Modern France: Eurasian Trade, Exoticism, and the Ancient Regime*. Oxford: BERG, 2008.

33 Charles Deulin 1878 suggests that the idea of the seven-leagued boots in *Le Petit Poucet* is probably taken from the ascent of Muhammad to Heaven. "la jument de Mahomet dont les enjambees s'etendaient aussi loin que la plus longue vue" (327) (Muhammad's mare that leapt and took him to the highest sky).

34 French travelers to the East in the seventeenth century included Jean Coppin (1615–90), Paul Chardin (1673–7), Jean-Baptiste Tavernier (1605–89), Jean de Thevenot (1633–67), Francois de La Boullaye-Le Gouz (1623–c. 1668), and Paul Lucas.

References

'Alf Layla Wa Layla [One Thousand and One Nights]'. Baghdad: Dar al-Tarbyah lil Tiba'ah wa'l-Nashir, n.d.

'Ayssa, Razuq. '"Asil al-'Adah Fi Qar" al-Tibul' Wa Daq al-Awani al-Nuhasiah Fi Khisuff al-Qamar''. *Al-Najim* 8 (1936): 49–52.

Aarne, Ancti, and Stith Thompson. *The Types of the Folktales: A Classification and Bibliography*. Helsinki: Suomalainen Tiedeakatemia, 1964.

Abdullmalik, Bin Hisham. *Al-Syrah al-Nabawyah*. Beirut: Dar Al Kitab Al-Arabi, 1990.

Abdulwahab, Sulayman. *Sharih Kitab Al-Tawhid*. Vol. 1. Riyadh: Maktabat Riyadh al-Hadithah, n.d.

Abu al-Fida', and Isma 'il bin 'Umar. *Tafsir Ibn Kathir*. Vol. i. Beirut: Dar al-Fikr, 1980.

al-'Abad, Isma'il. *al-Muhit fi 'l-Lughah [The Elaboration of Language]*. Vol. 5. Beirut: 'A lam al-Kutub, 1994.

al-'Abshihi, Shihabaldin Mohammed. *al-Mustatraf fi fann kull Mustazraf [The Humorous in all the Ludicrous Arts]*. Vol. 2. Beirut: Dar al-Kutub al-'Alamyah, 1983.

Al-'Attar, Farid Al-Din. *Mantiq Al-Tayr*. Edited by Badi' Mohammed Jum'ah (trans.). Beirut: Dar Al-Andalus lil Tiba'ah wa Al-Nashr, 2002.

al-'Abbadi, Muhammed Shamsulhaq. *'Uon al-Ma'bbud*. Vol. x. Beirut: Dar al-Kutub, 1994.

al-Abshihi, Shihabaldin Mohammed al-Mustatraf fi fann kull Mustazraf. *[The Humorous in all the Ludicrous Arts]*. Vol. 2. Beirut: Dar al-Kutub al-'Ala'myah, 1983.

al-A'drisi, Abu 'Abdullah al-Sharrif. *Nuzhat al-Mishtaq fi Akhtirraq al-Afaq*. Leiden: E.J. Brill, 1866.

al-'Aisami, 'Abdul Malik. *Samt al-Nujjum al-'Awalli fi Anbba' al-Awa'il wa al-Tawalli*. Vol. iii. Beirut: Dar Al Kutub Al A'lmiah, 2007.

al-Asbahani, Abi al-Sheikh. *al-'Adhamah*. Vol. v. Riyadh: Dar Al Asimah, 1987.

al-'Asqalani, Ahmed Abu al-Fahil. *Fatih 'l-Bari*. Beirut: Dar al-Ma'rifah, 1959.

al-Baghdadi, 'Abdul Qadir. *Khizanat al-Adab wa Lub Libab Lissan al-'Arab*. Vol. vii. Cairo: al-Hay'ah al-Maryiah al-'Amah lil Kitab, 1979.

Al-Baghdadi, 'abdul Qadir Bin Amr. *Khizanat Al-Adab Wa Lub Lubab Lisan Al-Arab*. Cairo: Maktabat Al-Khanji, 1996.

Al-Baghdadi, Isma'il Pasha. *Hidayat Al-'Arifin: Asma' Al-Mu'lifin Wa Athar Al-Musenifin*. Beirut: Dar ahya' Al-Turath Al-'Arabi, 1951.

al-Bakri, 'Abdulah bin 'Abdul'aziz. *Al-la'li' fi Sharih Amali al-Qali [The Pearls of the Interpretation of Amali Al-Qali]*. Poetry Encyclopedia. CD-ROM, 2001.

al-Ba'labaki, Munir, and Ruhi al-Ba'labaki. *al-Mawrid Dictionary: Arabic/English: English/Arabic*. Beirut: Dar al-'Ilim lil Malayin, 2006.

al-Bayhaqi, Ibrahim. *al-Mahasin wa 'l-Masawi' [The Advantages and Disadvantages]*. Beirut: Dar Beirut lil Nashir wa 'l-Tiba'ah, 1984.

Al-Brusaui, Isma'il Haqqi. *Tafsir Ruh Al-Bayan*. Constantinople: Matba'ah 'Uthmaniya, 1913.

Al-Dimashqi, Ibn Kathir. *Al-Bidayah Wa Al-Nihayah*. Beirut: 'Alam Al-Kutub, 2003.

al-Dimiri, Kamalludin bin Musa. *Hayat al-Haywan al-Kubra [The Long Life of the Animal]*. Cairo: Mustafa al-Babwi al-Halabi, 1978.

Al-Farahidi, 'abdul Rahman. *Al-'Ayn*. Beirut: Dar Maktabat Al-Hilal, 1986.

al-Hamawi, Yaqut. *Mu'jam al-Buldan [The Atlas of Countries]*. Vol. 11. Beirut: Dar Ahya' al-Turath al-'Arabi, 1988.

al-Hanafi, Yusuf Bin Musa. *Mu'tasar al-Mukhtasar*.' Alam al-Kutub, n.d.

al-Isfahani, Abu al-Faraj. *al-Aghani*. Vol. x & xxi. Tunisia: al-Dar al-Tunisyah lil Nashir, 1983.

al-Isfahani, Raghib. *Muhadarat al-Udaba' wa Muhawarat al-Shua'ra' wa 'l-bulagha [The Literati's Lectures and the Poets' and Rhetoricians' Dialogues]*. Vol. 4. Beirut: Dar Sadir, 2004.

al-Iskafi, Abu Abdullah. *Mukhtasar Kitab al-'Ayn [The Shortened Book of the "Well"]*. Vol. 2. Muscat: Ministry of National Heritage and Culture, 1998.

al-Jahidh, Abu 'Uthman. *Al-Hayawan [The Animal]*. Beirut: Dar Ahya' al-Turath al-'Arabi, 1969.

al-Jawhari, 'Ali. *Masnad Abi al-Ja'ad*. Vol. i. Beirut: Mu'sasat Nadir, 1990.

al-Jawzi, Abu al-Faraj. *al-A'dhkya'*. Vol. i. Poetry Encyclopedia/ Ibn al-Jawzi. CD-ROM, 2001.

al-Jawzi, Abu al-Faraj. *Zad al-Masir*. Vol. iii. al-Maktab al-Islami, 1983.

al-Jazri, Abu Sadat Mubarak. *al-Nihayah fi Gharib al-Athar*. Vol. iii. Beirut: al-Maktabah al-'Alamyah, 1979.

Al-Jubouri, Dhia A.H. *The Medieval Idea of the Saracen as Illustrated in English Literature, Spectacle and Sport*. PhD diss., University of Leicester, 1972.

Al-Juhayman, Abdul Karim. *Asatir Sha'byah Min Qalb Jazirat Al-'Arab (Popular Myths from the Heartland of Arabia)*. Beirut: Dar AI-Thaqafah, 1980.

al-Kufi, Abu Bakir 'Abdullah. *Musanaf Ibn Abi Shaybah*. Vol. v. Riyadh: Maktabat al-Rashid, 1988.

al-Ma'arri, Abu al-'Ala'. *Risalat al-Ghufran* Beirut: Maktabat al-Hilal, 1988.

al-Maghribi, Ibn Sa'id. *al-Jughrafiah*. Beirut: al-Maktab al-Tijari lil Tiba'ah wa 'l-Nashir, 1970.

al-Maliki, Ahmed Bin Ghanim. *al-Fawakih al-Dawani*. Vol. ii. Beirut: Dar al-Fikr, 1994.

al-Manawi, 'Abdul Ra'uf. *Fayd 'l-Qadir [The Graceful Abundance of God]*. Vol. 1. Cairo: al-Maktabah al-Tijaryah al-Kubra, 1945.

al-Mas'udi, 'Ali Bin al-husayn. *Muruj al-Dhahab*. Vol. ii. Beirut: Dar al-Kutub al-'Almyah, 1986.

al-Nawawi, Abu Zakarya Yahya. *Sharih al-Nawawi 'ala Sahih Muslim*. Beirut: Dar Ahya' al-Turath al-'Arabi, 1971.

al-Naysaburi, Abu al-Fahil. *Majma' al-Amthal*. Vol. i & ii. Beirut: Dar al-Ma'rifah, n.d.

al-Nimri, Abu Umar Yusif. *al-Tamhid li Ibn 'Abdulbar [The Preface of Ibn Abdul Bar]*. Vol. 16. Rabat: Ministry of Endowments and Religious Affairs, 1976.

Al-Nuiri, Shihab Al-Din. *Nihayat Al-'Arb Fi Fanun Al-'Adab*. Beirut: Dar Al-Kutub Al-'Almiya, 2004.

al-Qazwini, Zakarya. *Ija'ib al-Makhluqat wa Ghara'ib al-Mawjudat [The Wonders of Creatures and the Mysteries of Beings]*. Cairo: Mustafa al-Halabi, 1980.

al-Qurtubi, Abu'Abdullah Mohammed. *Tafsir al-Qurtubi*. Vol. 7. Cairo: Dar al-Sha'ab, 1964.

al-Qurtubi, Yusuf Ibn 'Abdulbar. *Bahjatal-Majalis wa Uns 'I-Majdlis wa Shahinn al-Dhihin wa 'I-Hajis*. Vol. ii. Beirut: Dar al-Kutub al-'Almyah, 1982.

al-Qushayri, Muslim Bin al-Hajaj. *Sahih Muslim*. Vol. iv. Beirut: Dar Ahya' al-Turath al-'Arabi, n.d.

Al-Rawi, Ahmed K. 'The Arabic Ghoul and Its Western Transformation'. *Folklore* 120, no. 3 (December 2009): 291–306.

al-Sajistani, Abi Dawud. *Sunan Abi Dawud*. Vol. iv. Beirut: Dar al-Fikr, n.d.

al-Shawkani, Muhammed 'Ali. *Nayl al-Awttar*. Vol. vii. Beirut: Dar al-Jil, 1973.

al-Siuti, 'Abdulrahman. *al-Dibaj 'ala Muslim*. Vol. v. Khubar: Dar Ibn 'Affan, 1996.

al-Tabari, Muhammed Bin Jarir. *Tafsir al-Tabari*. Vol. xxvii. Beirut: Dar al-Fikr, 1984.

al-Tahawi, Abu Ja'far. *Sharih Ma'ani al-Athar*. Vol. iv. 'Alam al-Kutub, 1994.

al-Tahawi, Abu Ja'far. *Sharih Mashkal al-Athar [The Interpretation of the Shaped Heritage]*. al-Maktabah al-Shamela (2.11). CD ROM, 2007.

al-Tamimi, Muhammed Bin Hayyan. *Sahih Ibn habban*. Vol. xiii. Beirut: Mu'sasat al-Risalah, 1967.

al-Tasturi, Sa'id bin Ibrahim. *al-Mudhakar wa 'l-Mu'anath [The Feminine and Masculine]*. 2001.

al-Tirmidhi, Muhammed. *Sunan al-Tirmidhi*. Beirut: Dar Ahya' al-Turath al-'Arabi, n.d.

al-Waqidi, Muhammed Bin 'Umar. *al-Maghazi*. Vol. i. Beirut: 'Alam al-Kutub, 1984.

Al-Zamakhshari, Abi Al-Qasim. *Rabi' al-Abrar wa Nusus al-Akhbar*. Dar Al-'Allami lil Matbu'at, 1992.

al-Zubaydi, Mohammed. *Taj 'l-'Arus min Jawahir al-Qamus [The Crown of the Bride from the Gems of the Dictionary]*. Vol. 30. Kuwait: al-Majlis al-Watani lil Thaqafah wa 'l-finun wa 'l-Adab, 1998.

Ali, Jawad. *Al-Mufassal Fi Tarikh al-'Arab Qabla al-Islam*. London: Dar Al Saqi, 2001.

Beaumont, Daniel. 'Introduction'. In *Alf Laylah Wa Laylah Or The 1001 Nights*, 2002. http://www.arabiannights.org/index2.html.

Beckford, William. *Vathek; Translated from the Original French: Third Edition, Revised and Corrected*, 3rd ed. London: W. Clarke, 1816.

Birkalan, Hande A. 'The Thousand and One Nights in Turkish'. *Fabula* 45, no. 3 (January 2004): 221–36.

Birrell, Anne. *Chinese Mythology: An Introduction*. Baltimore: Johns Hopkins University Press, 1993.

Bottigheimer, Ruth. 'Fairy Tales and Folk Tales'. In *International Companion Encyclopedia of Children's Literature*, edited by Peter Hunt, 261–74. Cornwall: Routledge, 2004.

Brontë, Charlotte. *Jane Eyre: An Autobiography*. London: Humphrey Milford, 1901.

Brontë, Emily. *Wuthering Heights: A Novel, by Ellis Bell, in Three Volumes*. Thomas Cautley Newby, 1847.

Burton, Richard Francis. *A Plain and Literal Translation of the Arabian Nights' Entertainment, Now Entitled The Book of the Thousand Nights and a Night; with Notes Anthropological and Explanatory*. London: The Burton Club, 1886–1888.

Burton, Richard. *The Book of the Thousand Nights and a Night: A Plain and Literal Translation of The Arabian Nights Entertainments*. London: The Burton Ethnological Society, 1885.

Burton, Richard Francis. *The Book of the Thousand Nights and a Night: With Introduction Explanatory Notes on the Manners and Customs of Moslem Men and a Terminal Essay Upon the History of the Nights*. London, 1885–8.

Burton, Richard Francis. *Personal Narrative of a Pilgrimage to Al-Madinah and Meccah*. Vol. 1. London: Tylson and Edwards, 1893.

Bushnaq, Inea. *Arab Folktales*. New York: Pantheon Books, 1986.

Carinci, Francesco, Scapoli, Luca, Palmieri, Annalisa, Zollino, Ilaria, and Pezzetti, Furio. 'Human Genetic Factors in Non-Syndromic Cleft Lip and Palate: An Update'. *International Journal of Pediatric Otorhinolaryngology* 10, no. 1016 (2007): 1–11.

Carpenter, Humphrey, and Prichard, Mari. *The Oxford Companion to Children's Literature*. Oxford: Oxford University Press, 1991.

Chauvin, Victor. *Bibliographie Des Ouvrages Arabes Ou Relatifs Aux Arabes, Publiés Dans l'Europe Chrétienne de 1810–1885*. Vol. 6. Liège: H. Vaillant-Carmanne, 1902.

Clements, William M., ed. *The Greenwood Encyclopedia of World Folklore and Folklife: Southeast Asia and India, Central and East Asia, Middle East*. Vol. II. Westport: Greenwood Press, 2006.

Cohen, Francis. 'Fairy Tales, or the Lilliputian Cabinet, Containing Twenty-Four Choice Pieces of Fantasy and Fiction'. *Quarterly Review* 21 (1819): 91–112.

Cosquin, Emmanuel. *Etudes folkloriques*. Paris: E. Champion, 1922.

Crapanzano, Vincent. *The Ḥamadsha: A Study in Moroccan Ethnopsychiatry*. Berkeley: University of California Press, 1973.

Crapanzano, Vincent. *Tuhami: Portrait of a Moroccan*. Chicago: University of Chicago Press, 1985.

Crapanzano, Vincent. *Imaginative Horizons: An Essay in Literary-Philosophical Anthropology*. Chicago: University of Chicago Press, 2003.

Darmesteter, James, ed. *The Zend-Avesta Part ii*. Oxford: The Clarendon Press, 1883.

Davis, Dick (trans.). *Shahnameh: The Persian Book of Kings*. London: Penguin Books, 2006.

De Gubernatis, Angelo. *Zoological Mythology or the Legends of Animals*. Vol. II. London: Trübner & Company, 1872.

Deulin, Charles. *Les Contes De Ma Mere L'Oye Avant Perrault*. Paris: E. Dentu, 1878.

Dew, Nicholas. 'The Order of Oriental Knowledge: The Making of d'Herbelot's Bibliotheque Orientale'. In *Debating World Literature*, edited by Christopher Prendergast and Benedict Richard, 233–52. London: Verso, 2004.

Dickens, Charles. *Christmas Stories from 'Household Words' and 'All the Year Round'*. London: Chapman and Hall Ltd, 1913.

d'Herbelot, Barthelemy d'. *Bibliothèque Orientale, Ou Dictionnaire Universel, Contenant Tout Ce Qui Fait Connaître Les Peuples de L'Orient: Tome 5*. Boston: Adamant Media Corporation, 2001.

Doughty, Charles M. *Travels in Arabia Deserta*. Vol. 2. Suffolk: Jonathan Cape, 1964.

Doughty, Charles M. *Travels in Arabia Deserta, with a New Preface by the Author*. Vol. I. London: Butler & Tanner Ltd, 1933.

Durayd, Ibn, and Abu Bakir. *Jamharat Al-Lughah [The Compilation of Language]*. Vol. 2. Beirut: Dar Al-'Ilim lil Malayin, 1987.

Duyvendak, Jan Julius Lodewijk. 'China's Discovery of Africa: Lectures Given at the University of London on January 22 and 23, 1947'. In *Probsthain's Oriental Series*. London: Arthur Probsthain, 1949.

Eberly, Susan Schoon. 'Fairies and the Folklore of Disability: Changelings, Hybrids, and the Solitary Fairy'. In *The Good People: New Fairylore Essays*, edited by Peter Narvez, 227–50. Kentucky: The University Press of Kentucky, 1991.

Elphinstone, Mountstuart. *An Account of the Kingdom of Caubul and Its Dependencies in Persia, Tartary, and India*. Vol. 1. London: Richard Bentley, 1839.

El-Shamy, Hasan. *Folk Traditions of the Arab World: A Guide to Motif Classification*. Vol. 1. Bloomington: Indiana University Press, 1995.

El-Shamy, Hasan. 'Oral Traditional Tales and the Thousand Nights and a Night: The Demographic Factor'. In *The Telling of Stories: Approaches to a Traditional Craft*, edited by Morton Nøjgaard et al., 63–117. Odense: Odense University Press, 1990.

El-Shamy, Hasan. *Religion Among the Folk in Egypt*. Westport: Praeger, 2008.

El-Shamy, Hasan. *Tales Arab Women Tell and the Behavioral Patterns They Portray*. Bloomington: Indiana University Press, 1999.

El-Shamy, Hasan. *Types of the Folktale in the Arab World: A Demographically Oriented Tale-Type Index*. Bloomington: Indiana University Press, 2004.

'Encyclopaedia of Islam'. Leiden: E.J. Brill, 1997.

Firdausi. *The Shah Nameh*. Edited by James Atkinson (trans.). London: George Routledge and Sons, Limited, 1892.

Galland, Antoine (trans.). *Arabian Nights Entertainments: Consisting of One Thousand and One Stories, Told by the Sultaness of the Indies / Translated into French from the Arabianmss. by M.Galland...and Now Made English from the Last Paris Edition*. Vol. 4. London: T. N. Longman (Cambridge Univ. Library), 1718.

Galland, Antoine. *Les Mille et Une Nuits, Tome Troisième*. Paris: Garnier frères, 1949.

Gaskell, Elizabeth. *Cranford; A Tale*. London: J. M. Dent & Sons, 1914.

Giles, Herbert. *Chuang Tzu: Mystic, Moralist, and Social Reformer*. London: Bernard Quaritch, 1889.

Goldberg, Christine. 'The Dwarf and the Giant (AT327B) in Africa and the Middle East'. *Journal of American Folklore* 116, no. 461 (2003): 339–50.

Gordon, Lucie Duff. *Letters from Egypt: Lady Duff Gordon's Letters from Egypt*. London: R. B. Johnson, 1902.

Gorton, T.J. 'Arabic Influence on the Troubadours: Documents and Directions'. *Journal of Arabic Literature* 5 (1974): 11–16.

Gray, Louis H. 'Fifteen Prakrit-Indo-European Etymologies'. *Journal of the American Oriental Society* 60, no. 3 (1940): 361–69.

Green, Thomas A. *Folklore: An Encyclopedia of Beliefs, Customs, Tales, Music, and Art*. Vol. 1. California: ABC-CLIO, 1997.

Grimm, Wilhelm. *Kinder Und Hausmaerchen*. Vol. I. Berlin: Reimer, 1812.

Grimm, Wilhelm, and Margaret Hunt (trans.). *Kinder Und Hausmaerchen*. London, 1884.

Habibi, Amil. *Saraya Bint Al-Ghoul*. London: Ryah al-Rayes, 1992.

Haddawy, Husain Tra. *The Arabian Nights*. New York: Alfred A. Knopf, 1992.

Hamadi, Salih Bin. *Qusas Shabiah Tunisiah' in Dirassat Fi al-Issatir Wa 'l-Mu'taqadat [Studies in Myths and Beliefs]*. Tunisia: Dar Busalamah lil Tiba'ah wa 'l-Nashir, 1983.

Hanauer, J.E. *Folk-Lore of the Holy Land: Moslem, Christian and Jewish*. London: Duckworth & Co, 1907.

Hashim, Bin Sa'id, and Bin Muhammed Hashim. *Al-Ashbah Wa al-Naha'ir Fi Ash'ar al-Mutaqadimin Wa al-Jahlyinn al-Mukhahramin*. Poetry Encyclopedia/Hashim, 2001.

Holt, Peter M., and Ann Katherine Holt. *The Cambridge History of Islam*. Cambridge: Cambridge University Press, 1997.

Ibn Kathir, Abi Al-Fida'. *Al-Bidayah Wa al-Nihayah*. Beirut, 1988.

Ibn Mandhur, Mohammed. *Mukhtasar Tarikh Dimashqq Li Ibn 'Asakkir*. Vol. xxvii. Damascus: Dar al-Fikr, 1990.

Ibn Mandhur, Mohammed Bin Makram. *Lissan Al-'Arab*. Beirut: al-Maktabah al-'Alamyah, 2005.

Irwin, Robert. *The Arabian Nights: A Companion*. New York: I. B. Tauris, 2004.

Jung, C.G. 'The Symbolic Life'. In *The Collected Works* (trans. R.F.C. Hull). London: Routledge and Kegan Paul, 1977.

The Jewish Encyclopedia. *Dragon*. Vol. 4. New York, 1901–1906.

Kane, Robert. 'James Crossley, Sir Thomas Browne, and the Fragments on Mummies'. *R. E. S.* 9, no. 35 (1933): 266–74.

Kimpton, Jen. 'Jean-Baptiste Adanson (1732–1804): A French Dragoman in Egypt and the Near East'. In *Travelers in the Near East*, edited by Charles Foster, 71–103. London: Stacey International & ASTENE, 2006.

Kirby, W.F. '"Appendix II: Contributions to the Bibliography of the Thousand and One Nights, and Their Imitations, with a Table Showing the Contents of the Principal Editions and Translations of the Nights".' In *A Plain and Literal Translation of the Arabian Nights' Entertainment, Now Entitled the Book of the Thousand Nights and a Night*, edited by Richard F. Burton. London: The Burton Club, 1886.

Lane, Edward William. *An Account of the Manners and Customs of Modern Egyptians: Written in Egypt During the Years 1833, –34, and –35*. London: John Murray, 1860.

Lane, Edward William. *An Arabic-English Lexicon, Part 6*. Beirut: Librairie Du Liban, 1980.

Lane, Edward William. *Arabian Society in the Middle Ages: Studies from the Thousand and One Nights*. London: Curzon Press, 1987.

Lane, Edward William. *The Thousand and One Nights, Commonly Called in England the Arabian Nights Entertainments*. Vol. 3. London: Routledge, Warne & Routledge, 1865.

Lang, Andrew, ed. *Perrault's Popular Tales*. Oxford: Clarendon Press, 1888.

Lang, Andrew, ed. *The Arabian Nights Entertainments: Selected and Edited by Andrew Lang*. London: Longmans, Green, and Co, 1929.

Larzul, Sylvette. 'Further Considerations on Galland's Mille et une Nuits: A Study of the Tales Told by Hanna'. *Marvels & Tales: Journal of Fairy-Tale Studies* 18, no. 2 (2004): 258–71.

Lindemans, Micha F. 'Gallu. Encyclopedia Mythica. Encyclopedia Mythica Online'. 2008 (1997). http://www.pantheon.org/articles/g/gallu.html.

Lisan Al-'Arab [The Arabic Tongue]. Vol. 3 & 4. Beirut: al-Maktabah al-'Alamyah, 2005.

Mackenzie, Donald A. *Myths of Babylonia and Assyria*. London: The Gresham Publishing Company, 1910.

Mahdi, Muhsin. *The Thousand and One Nights*. Leiden: E. J. Brill, 1995.

Marchant, E.C. 'Richardson, Charles (1775–1865), Rev. John D. Haigh'. In *Oxford Dictionary of National Biography*. London: Oxford University Press, 2004.

Ma'ruf, Bashar, Abu al-Ma'ati al-Nuri, Aymen al-Zamili, Ahmed 'Ayed, and Mahmud Khalil. *al-Masnad al-Jami'*. Vol. iv and vi. Beirut: Dar al-Jil, 1996.

Marzolph, Ulrich, and Richard van Leeuwen. *The Arabian Nights Encyclopedia*. Vol. II. ABC CLIO, 2004.

McElroy, Colleen J. *Over the Lip of the World: Among the Storytellers of Madagascar*. Washington, DC: University of Washington Press, 2001.

Menocal, Maria Rosa. *The Arabic Role in Medieval Literary History: A Forgotten Heritage*. Philadelphia: University of Pennsylvania Press, 1987.

Mercatante, Anthony S. *The Facts on File Encyclopedia of World Mythology and Legend*. New York: Facts on File, 1988.

Mitra, Kalipadra. 'The Bird and Serpent Myth'. *The Quarterly Journal of the Mythic Society* 16 (1925–6): 189.

Montagu, Mary Wortley. *Letters*. New York: Alfred A. Knopf, 1992.

Moore, Thomas. *Lallah Rookh (1890): An Oriental Romance*. New York: T.Y. Crowell & Co, n.d.

Muhawi, Ibrahim, and Sharif Kanaana. *Speak Bird, Speak Again: Palestinian Arab Folktales*. Berkley: University of California Press, 1989.

Murphy, G. Ronald. *The Owl, the Raven, and the Dove*. Oxford: Oxford University Press, 2000.

New World Private School. 'Sindbad & the Rukh Bird'. 2012. https://www.youtube.com/watch?v=t9PCxV9KdWk.

Olasoji, H.O., V.I. Ugboko, and G.T. Arotiba. 'Cultural and Religious Components in Nigerian Parents' Perceptions of the Aetiology of Cleft Lip and Palate: Implications for Treatment and Rehabilitation'. *British Journal of Oral and Maxillofacial Surgery* 45 (2007): 302–5.

Opie, Iona Archibald, and Peter Opie. *The Classic Fairy Tales*. Oxford: Oxford University Press, 1992.

'Oxford English Dictionary Online'. 1989, 2000, 2004, and 2008. 'S.v. "carcass" & "Rukh"'. In *The Oxford English Dictionary*, 1989.

Perho, Irmeli. 'The Arabian Nights as a Source for Daily Life in the Mamluk Period'. *Studia Orientalia* 85 (1999): 139–62.

Perrault, Charles. *The Tales of Mother Goose*, trans. Charles Welsh. New York: D. C. Heath & Co. 1901.

Perrault, Charles. *Les Hommes Illustres Qui Ont Paru En France Pendant Ce Siecle*. Edited by D.J. Culpin. Tiibingen: Gunter Narr, 2002.

Polo, Marco. *The Travels of Marco Polo the Venetian*. London: J. M. Dent & Sons LTD, 1914.

Potter, J.W. 'Chinese-East African Trade Before the 16th Century'. *Ufahamu: A Journal of African Studies* 5, no. 2 (1974): 113–34.

Reynolds, Dwight F. *Arab Folklore: A Handbook*. Westport: Greenwood Press, 2007.

Röhrich, Lutz. 'Dragon'. *Enzyklopädie Des Märchens* 3 (2003): 787–820.

Rose, Carol. *Giants, Monsters, & Dragons: An Encyclopedia of Folklore, Legend, and Myth*. New York: W. W. Norton.Routledge, 2001.

Sadan, Joseph. 'The Arabian Nights and the Jews'. In *The Arabian Nights Encyclopedia*, edited by Ulrich Marzolph and Richard van Leeuwen, 42–46. California: ABC CLIO, 2004.

Said, Edward. *Orientalism: Western Conceptions of the Orient*. London: Penguin, 2003.

Saintyves, P. *Les Contes de Perrault et Jes Recits Parallels*. Paris: Emile Nourry, 1923.

Scott, Walter. *Minstrels of the Scottish Border: Consisting of Historical and Romantic Ballads, Collected in the Southern Counties of Scotland; with a Few of Modern Date, Founded upon Local Tradition*. London: J. Ballantyne for T. Cadell and W. Davies, 1802.

Sengers, Gerda. *Women and Demons: Cult Healing in Islamic Egypt*. Translated by D.E. Orton. Leiden: Brill, 2003.

Shahi, Ahmed, and F.C.T. Moore. *Wisdom from the Nile*. Oxford: Clarendon Press, 1978.

Shosha, Boaz. 'Review of Social Life and Popular Culture'. In *The Arabian Nights Encyclopedia*, edited by Ulrich Marzolph and Richard van Leeuwen, 50–54. ABC CLIO, 2004.

Skeat, Walter W. 'Caoutchouc'. *Notes and Queries, S. 11-II* 28 (1910): 25.

Smith, Byron Porter. *Islam in English Literature*. New York: Caravan Books, 1977.
Soriano, Marc. *Les Contes de Perrault: Culture Savante et Traditions Populaires*. Paris: Gallimard, 1968.
Sulayman. *Sharih Kitab al-Tawh'id*. Vol. i. Riyadh: Maktabat al-Riya' al-Hadithah, n.d.
Sumerian Mythology: A Study of Spiritual and Literary Achievement in the Third Millennium BC, 1961.
Sutherland, D.R. 'The Language of the Troubadours and the Problem of Origins'. *French Studies* 3, no. 10 (1956): 199–215.
Tatar, Maria. *The Hard Facts of the Grimms' Fairy Tales*. Princeton: Princeton University Press, 2003.
Thompson, Stith. *Motif-Index of Folk-Literature*. Vol. 2. Copenhagen: Rosenkilde and Bagger, 1956.
Thompson, Stith. *Motif-Index of Folk-Literature: Index A-K: A Classification of Narrative Elements in Folktales, Ballads, Myths, Fables, Mediaeval Romances, Exempla, Fabliaux, Jest-Books, and Local*. Bloomington: Indiana University Press, 2002.
Trinquet, Charlotte. 'On the Literary Origins of Folkloric Fairy Tales: A Comparison between Madame d'Aulnoy's "Finette Cendron" and Frank Bourisaw's "Belle Finette".' *Marvels & Tales: Journal of Fairy-Tale Studies* 21, no. 1 (2007): 34–49.
Uther, Hans-Jö. *The Types of International Folktales. A Classification and a Bibliography. Parts I–III*, n.d.
Warner, Marina. 'Mother Goose Tales: Female Fiction'. *Female Facts Folklore* 101 (1990): 3–25.
Westermarck, Edward. 'The Nature of the Arab Ginn, Illustrated by the Present Beliefs of the People of Morocco'. *The Journal of the Anthropological Institute of Great Britain and Ireland* 29, no. 3–4 (1899): 252–69.
West, E.W. (trans., ed). *Sacred Books of the East*. Vol. 24. Oxford: Oxford University Press, 1885.
Wittkower, Rudolph. '"Roc": An Eastern Prodigy in a Dutch Engraving'. *Journal of the Warburg Institute* 1, no. 3 (1938): 255–57.

2 The Rukh[1]

Introduction

Similar to the phoenix, the Rukh bird has captured the imagination of many Arab and Western writers and poets for centuries. The bird has been featured in a variety of contemporary stories, cartoons, video games, and films targeting young and adult readers and viewers. Examples include the famous Japanese cartoon *Sindbad Adventures* that was dubbed in Arabic and became popular in the Middle East in the 1980s in which the Rukh bird was frequently featured, as well as many Arabic YouTube videos that refer to the Rukh in various contexts. Most importantly, the ambiguity that surrounds this legendary bird adds to its fame because many readers maintain their curiosity surrounding understandings of the possible origins of this bird and its probable transformation. It is not unreasonable to assume that the bird will remain popular in people's imagination for many future decades as the Rukh has been associated with magic, wonder, power, and imagination. This chapter is focused on tracing the Chinese influences and Arabic origins of the Rukh by arguing that it is strongly connected to the Arabic "Anqa" and less linked to the Persian Simurgh or the legendary Indian Garuda birds. The chapter follows a critical approach in analyzing a variety of Arabic literary texts including the *Arabian Nights* and narratives embedded in various works. The study also relies on tracing and investigating the linguistic and cultural origins of various relevant words and terms that are linked to the Rukh's legend and literary understandings. It is important to note that Richard Burton's translation of the *Arabian Nights* is mostly cited here because it is regarded as the

> most complete version of texts relating to the *Arabian Nights* available in English. The first ten volumes with only minor alterations follow the text of the Calcutta II (Macnaghten) edition (1839–1842), which is commonly regarded as superior in wording to the Bulaq edition (nos. 1–262). The supplemental volumes add tales from various other sources.
>
> (Marzolph and van Leeuwen 2004, vol. ii: 508)

DOI: 10.4324/9781003462637-2

In the following section, a lexicographic discussion is presented on the Rukh through an examination of various Arabic dictionaries and sources.

Lexicon origins

The word "Rukh" has different spelling variations in English such as "Rukhkh," "Rookh," and "Roc." Originally, the word Rukh is Hindi (Rukkha in Prakrit), which means a forest, an isolated tree, or gleaming (*Oxford English Dictionary*, 1989; Gray 1940, 367–8). In Sanskrit and Persian, Rukh means "rook" which is taken from the game of chess. In Persia, the Rukh also refers to "face" (Burton 1885, vol. vi: 16–17) or the name of a region. al-Zubaydi 1998 said that Rukh is an area in Nishapur (2004, vol. vii: 256), and Al-Hamawi 1993a (c. 1178–c. 1225) confirmed that this region contained almost 300 villages that were all located within Khorasan (1993b, vol. iii: 311).

The first Arab lexicographers, such as Al-Farahidi (c. 718–c. 789), Al-Azhari (c. 895–c. 980), Ibn ‘abad (c. 936–c. 995), and Ibn Mandhur (c. 1311 d.), mentioned that the Rukh is originally a Persian word, and it stands for a tool used in a game, referring here to the rook in chess (Al-Farahidi 1986, vol. ix: 139; Al-Azhari 2001, vol. vi: 300; Ibn ‘Abad 1994, vol. iv: 172; Ibn Mandhur n.d., vol. iii: 1616). Al-Wahidi (c. 1075 d.) elaborates by saying that the word "Rukh" refers to a piece in chess, and is a "Persian word because Arabs in the old times and others who use the classical language never used it" (2009, vol. i: 339). In other words, the name of the Rukh bird was not derived from the abovementioned sources written by Arab lexicographers. Despite the efforts of the old lexicographers to compile all the known words, they did not refer to the Rukh as a bird because this meaning was not in circulation at that time. Also, the encyclopedic writer, Al-Jahidh (c. 776–c. 869), did not mention the Rukh in his voluminous book on zoology,[2] contrary to Marzolph and van Leeuwen's claim (2004, vol. ii, 694). In fact, the bird was only mentioned in later lexicons to mean a legendary bird. For example, Al-Zubaydi (1723–90) referred to it as a giant bird that can carry a rhinoceros. Al-Zubaydi confirmed that the Rukh is a loan word that has been Arabized (2004, vol. vii: 256).

The Rukh in Arabic sources

Different Muslim and Arab writers have discussed the Rukh in their various accounts, mostly related to their travels around the world. In this regard, the Rukh is mentioned in the *Encyclopaedia of Islam* 1997 as a bird first referenced by the Persian traveler Burzug Bin Shahriyar Al-Ramahirmizi (who lived in the tenth century) in *‘Aja’ib Al-Hind*, "The Wonders of India" (1908, vol. 8: 595). However, there is no direct reference to the Rukh in *‘Aja’ib Al-Hind*, based on a close reading of the text. Another work, entitled *Al-Sahih min Akhbar Al-Bihar wa 'aja'biha*, "The Right Accounts of the Seas and Their Wonders," written by the Persian Muslim writer Abi 'Umran Musa Al-Sirafi 2006 (c. 1009 d.) seems to be the source of the Rukh's tale in Al-Ramahirmizi's work.[3]

In this regard, Al-Sirafi cites a number of tales that refer to a giant bird which seems similar to the Rukh. For example, in one tale a group of men had their boat shipwrecked; most of them died, but seven of them found refuge on an island near India and remained there. On this island, a giant bird was found and was seen flying in the afternoon. Because the men were desperate, they decided that one of them would hold on to the bird's claws as it flew. Despite the danger, they believed that this was the only way they could survive because the men would either stay on the island and die or they would succeed in leaving it with the help of the bird. The first man who attempted this dangerous act managed to hide himself among the trees. By using tree bark, the man fastened himself to the bird's claws. As the bird flew away, the man landed on a mountain and stayed there until the second morning. He realized that he was in India after seeing a shepherd (Helpful roc. Type: 449/1511; B455.6). He realized that he was in an Indian village. Afterwards, his fellow friends followed the same strategy and were able to leave the island by landing in the same place (Al-Sirafi 2006: 54–6; Al-Ramahirmizi 1908, 1883–6: 12–14). There is another similar tale dealing with a man who originally came from Basrah. After being stranded on a remote island inhabited by savages, he also tied himself to the giant bird's claw and succeeded in departing the island. Unfortunately, the man was imprisoned again by another group of barbarians (Al-Sirafi 2006: 200; Al-Ramahirmizi 1908, 1883–6: 180–90). In this regard, Al-Qazwini's tale cited below, as well as "The Second Voyage" in "Sindbad the Seaman and Sindbad the Landsman" in the *Arabian Nights* (Burton 1885, vol. vi: 14–22), both have similar plots to the stories cited above.

Afterwards, more specifically in the twelfth century, there was another mention of the Rukh bird. Abi Hamid Al-Andalusi (c. 1169 d.) made the first reference to the word "Rukh" to denote the giant bird that we are familiar with today. He cited the story of the traveler 'Abdul Rahim Al-Sinni who found the quill of a Rukh's feather that was used as a water container. Al-Sinni mentioned that he got lost in the China Sea as strong winds drove his ship to a large and remote island. Upon waking up in the early morning, Al-Sinni and his fellow sailors saw on the horizon something glittering that looked like a dome. After approaching it, they found it was a giant egg (Mot. B31.1.1). The sailors started smashing it with their axes until they managed to break it open. When they noticed that there was a large bird chick inside the egg, they grabbed its feathers, which were not yet fully grown, and dragged the chick out of its shell. Afterwards, they prepared their pots and brought wood in order to cook the chick. After eating it, the sailors' white beards turned black, which was an indication that they had regained their youth (Mot. D0550). According to Al-Andalusi, the sailors became young again because they had used twigs that were fetched from the Tree of Youth; the twigs were used in stirring the pot in order to prepare their meal. On the next day, when the sailors woke up in the early morning, the mother Rukh bird had returned to its nest and found that its chick was gone. In reaction, the mother bird carried a big rock with its claw and chased the sailors as they continued on their sea journey. "The Rukh threw the rock at the men's ship, but Allah, the Merciful, saved them from its mischief" (Mot. B 31.1.2). As a souvenir, the sailors retained the bases of the chick's feathers, which they used as water containers due to their large size (2002: 77).

There were a number of other Muslim travelers who recounted similar stories including Al-Wardi (c. 1290/c. 1348). This writer merely made a slight change to the traveler's name, turning it into 'Abdul Rahman Al-Maghribi, which was later used in the *Arabian Nights* (Al-Wardi 1922, 76–7; Burton 1885, vol. v: 122–4 & "The Fifth Voyage of Sindbad the Seaman," vol. vi: 48–9; Chauvin 1902, vol. 6: 92–3).[4] Despite this slight change, we find that the tale cited in the *Arabian Nights* contains yet another different description from what Al-Andalusi mentioned in the original tale. For example, the *Arabian Nights* state that the men's gray hair turned black either due to heating the pot with "arrow-wood" or to eating the Rukh's meat (Burton 1885, vol. v: 124). These slight variations show how the original story changes over time depending on who is writing it down, yet the large similarities between the various Arabic texts and that of the *Arabian Nights* further suggest the strong influence of these works on the *Arabian Nights* tales. However, in order to clearly understand the Rukh's origin, we need to trace its historical and cultural connections.

The Rukh and its regional connections

A large number of Arab and oriental scholars have discussed the roots of the *Arabian Nights* for over two centuries. Some of them claimed that there were some Indian and Persian influences, but they either focused on the frame-story found in Indian tales or on the Persian background settings in other stories including the "names of the heroes, the geographical environment, and type of story" (Marzolph & van Leeuwen 2004, vol. ii: 603–4 and 672). In fact, there were some Indian works that were translated into Arabic such Ibn Al-Muqaffa's *Kalila wa Dimna* (c. 724/c. 759) wherein the Garuda bird was transformed into the Persian Simurgh. Afterwards, Al-Muqaffa converted the Persian bird into the "Anqa" that was known to his Arab readers (*Encyclopaedia of Islam* 1997, vol. 9: 615).

There are also references to older Persian books such as *Hezar Afsan*. The first Arab writer to mention the latter work was Al-Mas'udi (c. 957 d.), when he was discussing a work entitled *One Thousand and One Nights* whose Persian source was presumably *Hezar Afsan*, which means "thousand myths," and other popular works like *Farzah*, *Simas*,[5] and the *Book of Sindbad* (1973, vol. ii: 260). Also, Ibn al-Nadim (c. 998 d.), in his *Al-Fihrist*, mentioned that the Arabs translated from old Persian books many fables and stories like *Hezar Afsan*, but they "refined, revised, and edited" (1978, vol. i: 422) these works. The Muslim scribes used to delete any sections they considered non-Islamic or heathen found in the old tales to make them suitable for new Muslim readers. Hence, we find several important details or even plot elements missing in the newly formed tales. Ibn al-Nadim said that *Hezar Afsan* was a "boring and tedious" book (ibid.: 423), but he saw another work compiled by Al-Jahshiari that included different fabulous tales taken from the Persians, Arabs, and Byzantines, but its author died before finishing it (ibid.). As for *Hezar Afsan* it dealt with a king who killed a wife every night until he married a well-informed lady called Shehrazad who started narrating tales to him every night in order to avoid being killed (ibid.: 422–3). Finally, Al-Tawhidi (c. 1009 d.) referred to *Hezar Afsan* as an imaginary book that was both humorous and surprising since he viewed the events taking place in this book as impossible (n.d. vol. i: 23). In brief, there is evidence that the framework and some details found in a group of *Arabian Nights* tales are Persian or Indian, but this does not mean that all the other details are not related to the Arabs and their culture.

Before we discuss the Rukh itself, it is important to shed light on the other two legendary birds, the Garuda and the Simurgh, that are commonly believed to be associated with the Rukh. In relation to the Garuda, the *Mahabharata* and the *Ramayana* (III.39), Indian Sanskrit epics, mention this bird as a giant one that was able to carry elephants, which were held on its beak to be eaten, as well as being able to fight tortoises (De Gubernatis 1872: 94). This is the only – admittedly weak – link the Rukh has with the Garuda, as the Arabic "Anqa" bird is described in the same manner, as stated below. Later Indian writings, such as the eleventh-century *Kathasaritsagara*, describe a different bird "of the race of Garuda" but never mention its name. *Kathasaritsagara*, which means "Ocean of the Streams of Stories," contains Indian folk beliefs narrated by Somadeva. For example, the "Story of the Ancestors and Parents of Udayana King of Vatsa" stated that Mrigavati was bathing in a tank full of a blood-like liquid when a "bird of the race of Garuda suddenly pounced upon her and carried her off thinking she was raw flesh". Also, we learn in the "Story of Rupinika" that a "bird of the race of Garuda" unknowingly carried the body of an elephant in which a man was hiding. The giant bird "took it to the other side of the sea; there it tore open the elephant's hide with its claws, and, seeing that there was a man inside it, fled away". There are no clues suggesting that this bird "of the race of Garuda" was the Rukh itself. Although the evidence is weak, Mitra (1925–6: 189) suggested that the Rukh's origin could be traced back to the Indian Garuda. Wittkower agrees with Mitra, yet the former also suggests that the elephant carried by the Garuda bird could be a reference to a snake called Naga (1938: 255). In general, Mitra and Wittkower do not attempt to explain plenty of features of the Rukh that are still missing and have never been attributed to the Garuda. This includes the magical effects of the Rukh's feathers and chicks as well as the unique plot features of the Rukh's stories.

The other large bird, the Persian Simurgh (Mot. B31.5), was referred to by a number of Arab lexicographers, and they repeatedly blended its description with that of the Arabic "Anqa." For example, Al-Jahidh, Al-Tha'alibi (c. 961/c. 1037), and Al-Baghdadi explained the etymology of the Simurgh, saying that it is made up of "Si" and "Murgh" which both refer to "thirty birds" (al-Jahidh 1969, vol. vii: 120–1; Al-Tha'alibi 1985: 450; Al-Baghdadi 1996, vol. vii: 132–3). The similarity between the Simurgh and "Anqa" is also referenced in F. De Blois' claim, especially when a giant legendary bird is translated from a foreign language into Arabic (*Encyclopaedia of Islam*, 1997, vol. 9: 615).

Similar to the older account narrated by Al-Sadiq about the "Anqa" , the Persian poet Firdausi (c. 935–c. 1020) narrated the old history of Persia in his famous work the *Shahnameh* (Book of Kings) in which he mentioned the Simurgh in several places. For example, the mountain above which the Simurgh nested was called Alberz (Firdausi 1892, 49–50), which is reminiscent of Mount Qaf above which the "Anqa" bird resided. According to Firdussi, the mountain was so high that its peak reached the Pleiades. When Sam looked up, he "stared at the granite slopes, at the terrifying Simorgh, and at its fearsome nest, which was like a palace towering the clouds, but one not built by men's hands of from clay and water" (Davis 2006: 65). In the story of Zal, the son of Sam, we learn that he was abandoned on the mountain Alberz in order to be devoured by wild beasts. However, the Simurgh carried him in the air and protected him in its own nest similar to the "Anqa" in Al-Sadiq's tale. Here, the Simurgh rescued the baby by lifting it up and feeding it. In Arabic folktales, Hasan El-Shamy referred to many tales that included an eagle such as (Mot. 0554B*) "The Boy in Eagle's Nest" [Infant raised by bird] which is reminiscent of Firdausi's account (El-Shamy 2004: 1006). In another connection between the "Anqa" and the Simurgh that was later made after Islam, the Persian poet Farid Al-Din Al-'attar (c. 1142–c. 1220) mentioned that the Simurgh inhabited China and lived behind Mount Qaf (2002: 185 and 187).

The only strong link the Rukh had with the Simurgh was related to the magic feathers that they both possessed. In Zoroaster's sacred book, *The Zend-Avesta*, the Simurgh's feather was thought to give power and strength if someone rubbed his body with it. *The Zend-Avesta* mentioned the following in relation to the magic powers of the Simurgh:

> If a man holds a bone of that strong bird, or a feather of that strong bird, no one can smite or turn to flight that fortunate man. The feather of that

> bird brings him help; it brings unto him the homage of men, it maintains in him his glory.
>
> (1883: 241)

Furthermore, in Firdausi's *Shahnameh*, there is a reference in one of the tales to how Rustem's mother, the beautiful Rudabeh, gave birth to him. When the bird heard about her difficult labor, it instructed Zal to cut her and do the following: "Massage [milk and musk] into her wound, and you will see it heal within the day. After this, stroke her body with my feather, since its shadow will be auspicious" (Davis 2006: 105). Here, the Simurgh is thought to assist human beings in achieving miracles.

The other link with the Rukh is rather weak. In the Persian sacred book entitled "The Dina-i Mainog-i Khirad," the Simurgh was thought to reside and nest in a huge tree that looked like the Tree of Life because it produced an abundance of seeds that were picked up by another giant bird called the Kinamros. The seeds were later thrown into Earth with rain to give life (Chapter 62, verses 37–42) (West 1885: 113). This tree, however, is similar to the tree in al-Sadiq's tale on the "Anqa" and reoccurs in many other tales, so there is no strong evidence to suggest that the Rukh is linked to it. In the following section, a critical discussion of the "Anqa" and Rukh is presented to investigate the link between them.

The "Anqa" and Rukh

In Arabian mythology, the "Anqa" was a pre-Islamic giant bird with a human face and four wings. The bird used to live for 2,000 years and got married every 500 years. Its name was derived from its long white neck, and it was different from the phoenix firebird, though both of them originated in Arabia. It lived during the time of Moses and ate the animals around Jerusalem, but when Moses died, the bird flew to Nejd where it became extinct (al-Zamakhshari 1992: 418). There are conflicting stories on where the bird died.[6]

One of the earliest and most vivid accounts of the "Anqa" was narrated by Muhammed Ja'ffar Al-Sadiq (d. 818). Al-Sadiq's tale was written down by Abi Ishaq Al-Tha'labi, who quoted Abu Muhammed 'Abdullah Bin Hamid's book *Dala'il al-Nubwah* (n.d.: 326–31).[7] In this seemingly pre-Islamic tale, King Solomon, who lived several centuries before Christ, talked about fate and destiny with the birds, but the "Anqa" objected to this conviction. King Solomon defied the bird, saying: "Do you want to know what the strangest thing is?" The "Anqa" replied: "Yes." King Solomon explained:

> Tonight, a boy was born in the west, and a girl was born in the east. Both of them are the offspring of kings who will meet to fornicate in the safest place on earth, on one of the islands in the midst of the sea. This is all done by God's will.

The "Anqa" felt surprised and questioned Solomon about their true names. The bird announced: "Thou Prophet of God, I'll separate between them and will overthrow fate" (Tha'labi n.d.: 326). The owl supported the "Anqa" in its attempt.

The "Anqa," which was as large as a "camel with a human face, fingers, hands, and woman's breasts," flew to search for the girl (Tha'labi n.d.: 326). Finally, the giant bird saw the baby and snatched her away to a

> very high mountain in the middle of the sea where an island was located. On this mountain, there was a very high tree. Even birds cannot reach it unless they try very hard. The tree contained thousands of boughs, and each one was as big as a regular tree on earth with plenty of leaves.
> (Tha'labi n.d.: 326)

The "Anqa" placed the baby girl in the nest, which was very spacious, and breastfed her (Mot. B0201.1.1). It also provided her with all kinds of food and protected her from the cold and heat. In fact, this majestic tree will be mentioned several times in different contexts and is most likely the Tree of Life that later became associated with the Rukh bird.

In the meantime, the boy grew up and became a strong king who loved hunting. As he was fed up with hunting on the land, he decided to try the sea, so he prepared many ships and sailed away with his men. While they were in the middle of the sea, God sent His wind and the ships drifted away toward the "Anqa" and the girl, who were as far away as 50 years' sailing. The king looked around and saw a huge mountain in the midst of the sea above which was a huge tree. The tree's trunk was white, producing an aroma of chrysanthemum flowers. Each leaf was as large as an elephant's ear. The king was astonished by the scene he saw and became more curious to see the island, so he ordered his men to land. As the king went around the place, he saw no trace of human beings. The girl was looking down at the ships but could not understand what they were since she had not seen anything like them in her life. When the king and the girl finally saw each other, they felt surprised and at once fell in love. The girl, who considered the bird her mother, wanted to be with the king, but she was confined in a high place. The king thought of a way out and suggested:

> I'll slaughter my horse and disembowel it. I'll then enter its body and throw it on board my ship. When the "Anqa" returns, tell her that you see on board that thing [the ship] something strange which you want to look at.
> (Tha'labi n.d.: 329)

As planned, the "Anqa" snatched the horse's corpse and carried the king inside it to the girl who said: "My mother, how nice it is!" and she laughed, after which the bird flew away. The boy left the horse's corpse and entertained the girl for a while. "He touched her, deflowered her, and made her pregnant on the same day" (Tha'labi n.d.: 329). The tale ends with King Solomon's reminder that no one and nothing can stop God's will. On the other hand, the "Anqa" felt agitated and lost, so it flew away "toward the west and disappeared in one of the Western seas and promised not to show itself again" (al-Nuiri 2004, vol. xiv: 72). This was probably why the bird was called "Anqa" Maghrib (west). As for the owl, it felt ashamed too, so it hid among the mountains and wildernesses and promised not to show itself to the others in day the time (al-Nuiri 2004, vol. xiv: 73). Despite the importance of this tale, it has been ignored by scholars; it is both related to the Rukh and parts of the *Arabian Nights* tales such as the "Second Voyage of Sindbad the Seaman" and the "Third Qalandar's Tale."

Other descriptions of the "Anqa" are relevant here because they are associated with the Rukh. The bird is described, for example, by al-Baghdadi (c. 1621–c. 1682) in a detailed manner. He elaborates by saying that the egg of "Anqa" is as big as a mountain (1951: 134), which is a similar description to the Rukh's egg. Also, it was stated that the "Anqa" was the "largest bird snatching elephants like a kite snatches a mouse" (Al-Dimiri 1978, vol. ii: 87; al-Qazwini 1980: 281), which is also typically applied to the way the Rukh used to eat, according to some travelers mentioned below. Al-Dimiri further mentioned that the "Anqa" was hunted by following a trick in the sense that a large wagon would be placed amid two bulls. Then, heavy stones were put on the wagon in order to increase its weight and a man carrying fire would hide somewhere in the wagon. When the "Anqa" descended to snatch the bulls, it would not be able to lift them because of the weight, and then the man would appear and burn its wings (al-Dimiri 1978, vol. ii: 87).

Finally, al-Qazwini (c. 1203–c. 1283) mentioned that the "Anqa" used to hunt only elephants, huge fish, and dragons. "When it flies, one hears a sound of torrent or that of a wind blowing through trees" (1980: 281). Once, some merchants were sailing in the ocean. When they lost their way, they felt perplexed. "Suddenly, total darkness fell like a black cloud in the sky. The sailors asserted it was the 'Anqa', so we followed it until we became underneath the black spot. Then, we started praying until it disappeared" (al-Qazwini 1980: 281). Like the Rukh, the "Anqa" was believed to attack sailing ships in the sea. In the following section, a critical discussion is provided on the possible Chinese influences on the Arabic Rukh bird.

The Chinese influences on the Rukh

Though Marco Polo did not claim to see the Rukh himself, he narrated what Arab navigators described as a giant bird that appeared near the island of Madagascar (Polo 1914, 394).[8] He revealed that the Rukh used to appear at a certain time of the year, and it looked like an "eagle"; however,

> it is incomparably greater in size; being so large and strong as to seize an elephant with its talons, and to lift it into the air, from whence it lets it fall to the ground, in order that when dead it may prey upon the carcass.
>
> (Polo 1914, 393)

Hence, the eagle and Rukh seem to look identical as they seem to share the same qualities.

Other travelers like Ibn Battutah (c. 1304–c. 1377) stated that the bird had the reputation of attacking ships whenever it saw them. Previous studies emphasized the link between the Persian Simurgh and the Rukh, but this chapter argues that the Rukh was influenced by Chinese mythology, especially by the P'eng bird, where the Arabs' oral tradition is indirectly associated with the Rukh through a number of traditional practices and rituals popular in the early twentieth century. Further, the chapter provides textual evidence that assists in further understanding some *Arabian Nights* tales.

As will be explained below, some of the Arabic tales that refer to the Rukh are linked to the moon eclipse and can be seen in older popular practices widely spread in several parts of the Arab world up to the early twentieth century. For example, among the folklore traditions in Iraq was a popular habit of beating drums during a moon eclipse. People used to beat copper plates, bang on cooking pots, and even fire shots when there was an eclipse thinking that a whale had devoured the moon. In order to frighten the imaginary sea animal, they used to sing songs accompanied by drum beats when it became dark, and they continued until the moon appeared once more al-'Alwaji 1962, 4–7; 'Ayssa 1936, 49–52; al-'Ani 1985, 217; Al-Sudani, 1990, 53–4). The popular song goes like this:

> *Ya Huttah Ya Manhuttah*
> *Hiddi Kkumarrnah al-'Ali*
> *Ha<u>dh</u>a Kkumarrnah Anrridah*
> *Huwa 'Alinah <u>Gh</u>ali*
> *Wa Ann Kan ma Tihhddinah*
> *Ann Dugglich bil Siniaey*
>
> *Thy whale, thy engraved one,*[9]
> *Let go of our high moon.*
> *This is our moon that we want,*
> *and is very dear to us.*
> *If you don't let go,*
> *we'll bang on the tray.*

In fact, this cultural habit is found in other Arabic regions such as Oman. For example, some people in Dhofar who speak the al-Shahri language cast stones at unbreakable plates when there is an eclipse until the moon returns to its normal shape (al-Shahri 2000, 316). Hence, the habit of beating drums to frighten whales is rooted in some parts of Arabic culture whether that of the common people or seafarers.

The discussion offered above focused on the numerous sources that testify to the Arabic origins of the Rukh bird; however, there is also textual evidence that Chinese elements influenced the perception and concept of the Rukh, as will be discussed below. In Chinese mythology and the early philosophy of Taoism, the old folk stories of Chuang Tzu (399–295 BCE) are relevant here as they contain a reference to the P'eng mythical bird. In the story of the "Transcendental Bliss" (1–11), the following account is given:

> In the northern ocean there is a fish, called the Leviathan, many thousand li in size. This leviathan changes into a bird, called the Rukh, whose back is many thousand li in breadth. With a might effort it rises, and its wings obscure the sky like clouds.
>
> (Giles, 1889, 1)

Here, the giant fish that is called K'un was metamorphized into a great bird (Birrell 1993, 191). In this context, Herbert Giles, Chuang Tzu's translator, preferred to call the bird Rukh instead of P'eng probably to make the meaning clearer to his Western readers. Further, a Chinese traveler called Chou Ch'ü-fei went to Madagascar and wrote down the details of his travel in the year 1178, and he referred to a similar bird in his writing, stating:

> When they fly they obscure the sun for a short time. There are wild camels, and if the p'éng birds meet them, they swallow them up. If one finds a feather of the p'éng bird, by cutting the quill, one can make a water jar of it.
>
> (Duyvendak 1949, 22)

By examining the above account, Joshua Potter believes that the P'eng bird mentioned here "is most likely the rukh" (1974, 121). One of the main qualities of this mythical bird is "immortality and longevity" as it was believed that "'it received the gift of eternal life' from God" (Birrell 1993, 187). Indeed, the descriptions given above are identical to the accounts mentioned in the *Arabian Nights* and repeatedly stated by Arab travelers describing the Rukh, as will be discussed below.

It is important here to refer to one of the first Arabic accounts that made an indirect reference to this mythical bird. In his discussion of Gargizia near Mongolia, al-Beiruni (c. 973–c. 1048) talked about a giant bird that the locals called Khatu. He narrates a story told by a fellow traveler who accompanied some men in the wilderness of China, saying that once the sun darkened all of a sudden, all the travelers descended from their animals and knelt imitating the posture of worship. Upon observing the incident, the fellow man mimicked the other travelers until the sunlight appeared again. When he asked them about the event, the travelers ignorantly referred to a giant bird that dwelt in uninhabited wildernesses overseas that lay beyond China and Africa, and that fed on wild elephants. The travelers revealed that the bird used to eat its food like a rooster picking wheat seeds. They called it *Khatu*, which is a name given to a person held in high esteem such as the titles bestowed upon a Khan or leader (2007, vol. i, 89) in China.

As discussed above, the first mention of the word "Rukh" to mean giant bird came from Abi Hamid al-Andulusi (c. 1169 d.). In al-Sinni's tale, al-Andulusi's 2003 account coincided with that cited above by the Chinese traveler, Chou Ch'ű-fei. al-Sinni, whose tale is cited above, has a surname which reveals that he is originally from China. al-Sinni's description is identical to the account given above about the P'eng's quill which provides some evidence for the Rukh's Chinese origins (Duyvendak 1949, 22).

Other travelers and navigators narrated the same story such as al-Wardi (c. 1290–c. 1348) who only changed the name of the traveler, making him 'Abdul Rahman al-Maghribi, the name used in the *Arabian Nights* (al-Wardi 1922, 76–7; Burton 1885, vol. v, 122–4 & "The Fifth Voyage of Sindbad the Seaman," vol. vi, 48–9; Chauvin 1902, vol. 6, 92–3).[10] However, some details in al-Andulusi's tale were changed. For instance, the *Arabian Nights* mentioned that the reason why the gray hair of the old men turned black was either because the cooking pot was heated with "*arrow-wood*"[11] or because the men ate the Rukh's meat (Burton 1885, vol. v, 124).

Further, a similar tale was cited in another work, but this time the bird was not named and was presented to be as large as a bull. When the men killed the bird and ate its flesh, all their hair fell out in the beginning, but it grew black after five days and its color never changed again, indicating that they regained their youth (al-Sirafi 2006 128–9; al-Ramahirmizi 1908, 99–100). Again, this is another clear indication that the Rukh is the P'eng Chinese bird which is associated with "immortality and longevity" (Birrell 1993, 187). However, when al-Ansari (c. 1256–c. 1327), al-Dimiri (c. 1341–c. 1405), and al-Brusaui (c. 1653–c. 1724) quoted al-Andulusi, they did not mention the Tree of Youth which is, in fact, the core element of the tale; instead, they focused on the Rukh and the attack that occurred at sea (al-Ansari 1923, 161–2; al-Brusaui 1913, vol. xiv, 64). al-Dimiri changed al-Andulusi's reference to the Tree of Youth into arrow-tree despite the fact that he claimed that he took the story from its original source (1978, vol. i, 524). Additionally, al-Abshihi (c. 1388–c. 1446) changed the Tree of Youth into the wood of youth (al-Abshihi 1965, vol. ii, 113), a change that was due to the fact that Muslim scribes and writers used to delete any non-Islamic elements from manuscripts. In fact, the old belief in the Tree of Youth that exists on Earth dates back to Sumerian times, and Islam rejected such ideas. In brief, the scribes who collected the tales borrowed al-Wardi's and al-Dimiri's versions, which means that the tale was not introduced into the *Arabian Nights* earlier than the late fourteenth century.

Other stories that involve a Rukh-like bird are numerous in some medieval Arabic travel accounts. For example, one account describes a certain bird that was caught in Africa after hunting an elephant and eating almost a quarter of its body. The monarch ruling the region took some parts of the bird such as its feathers, claws, and beak. One of its feathers was as large as two goatskin containers (al-Sirafi 2006 97; al-Ramahirmizi 1908, 178). One of the feathers was two arms long, and the other one was large enough to be filled with water equal to 25 containers (al-Ramahirmizi 1908, 62 & 99). Also, al-Abi mentioned that a traveler saw on board his ship a sea bird with one elephant in its beak, another on its neck, and in each claw an elephant, and under its wing a rhinoceros, carrying all of them to its chicks to feed them (2004, vol. vi, 340). Furthermore, *Suar al-Aqalim* or *Haft Kishur*, which was written around 1347, agrees with the above accounts and adds other details about the Rukh:

> It is a giant creature and is enemy to the elephant and the rhinoceros. When it finds a chance, it clasps its claws into their bodies to carry them to a very high point in the sky so that the sun heat blinds them and makes their fat melt.
>
> (Mot. J 1813.12.2)

Afterward, the Rukh descends and feeds these animals to its chicks (Cited in al-Sirafi 2006, 97).

The other reference to the Rukh was made by the famous Arab traveler, Ibn Battutah. On his travel with others from China to Jawa Island, he mentioned that they lost their way at sea after sailing for 42 days, so some of the sailors wanted to return to China. But on the 43rd day, they saw a big mountain in the midst of the sea. Only 20 miles separated their ship from the mountain and the wind was still blowing and pushing the ship toward it. The other sailors felt surprised and beseeched God to save them from the danger. In the morning, Ibn Battutah and his men saw the mountain getting higher into the sky and sunlight appeared between the sea and the object. The sailors started crying and bade farewell to each other because they knew that what appeared to be the mountain was, in fact, the Rukh which would normally destroy ships at sea. Fortunately, the bird did not see the men and their approaching ship; thus, they were glad to stay alive (Ibn Battutah 1904, vol. ii, 209).

In relation to the Rukh's feather, it was known that the bird had huge precious quills that were sold in different markets. In his description of Qamar Island (Moon) which is also called Malay Island, located in the Bay of Bengal, al-Ansari said that the Rukh was often seen hovering there, especially on its eastern side:

> The residents regularly find its black feathers which they used like a goatskin container. The length of the feather, which was as thick as a finger, was about the size of a human being and the width of its shaft was about 15 cm.

The author revealed that some tradesmen used to take such feathers to Aden in Yemen to sell them and they were called Rukh's feathers (al-Ansari 1923, 161). Also, Polo narrated how some men who went on an expedition returned to China and presented to Kublai Khan a feather of the Rukh which "measured ninety spans, and the quill part to have been two palms in circumference" (Polo 1914, 393).

In brief, almost all of the above tales about the Rukh were linked to China and to the P'eng mythical bird. al-Brusaui, Ibn Battutah, and al-Ansari's assertions that the bird was first found in regions or islands near China, and the *Arabian Nights*' reference to its presence in China are just a few examples cited above. Additionally, al-Beiruni's account of the Chinese Khatu bird, al-Andulusi's first reference to the Rukh that was taken from a Chinese Muslim traveler, Chou Ch'ű-fei's account of the same bird, and the fact that several basic features are similar to those of the Rukh all suggest that the name of the Rukh and some of its features were derived from China. Most importantly, the Rukh's qualities that are associated with immortality, longevity, and large quills provide clear evidence that the P'eng mythical bird is the Rukh's origin. In the following section, a discussion of the Arab oral tradition is provided and some oral accounts that are associated with the Rukh are explained in order to trace the other historical and cultural associations attached to the Rukh.

Arabic oral tradition

Dwight Reynolds asserts in his work on Arabic folklore that the oral tradition plays an integral part in the lives of the Arabs, saying that "Arab culture … is permeated and held together in many different ways by its folklore" (2007, 26). Indeed, by studying the oral heritage of the Arab cultures, one can understand the nature of the society and the people. Even the *Arabian Nights* is believed to be a collection of oral tales (El-Shamy 1990, 77–9) that were later written down by different scribes throughout the previous centuries. It is important to note here that a few other tales that deal with the Rukh contain references to a number of popular practices and rituals which were practiced until recently in some parts of the Arab world, as highlighted above and elaborated on below.

In one of the tales cited by al-Qazwini who quoted the author of *'Aja'ib al-Bahar* (The Wonders of the Sea) (1980),[12] a man from Isfahan was in debt and could not earn a living for his family, so he decided to leave his city and travel by sea with some merchants. But the strong sea waves in the Persian Gulf pushed them to a dangerous narrow strait called Dardur.[13] The other merchants gathered around the captain of the ship and asked: "Is there any chance we can survive?" To which the captain replied: "It is only with Allah's will that we will be able to get through Dardur, but if someone would step down from the ship, I would do my best to save you." The Isfahani man said:

"Thou fellows, we are all in peril, and I'm a man tired of toiling; I had wished to die a long time ago." Turning to some travelers from Isfahan, he said: "If you swear you'll pay my debts and be benevolent toward my children, I'll sacrifice myself for your sake." The people from Isfahan agreed, so the man asked for instructions. The captain pointed to a nearby island that was located within three nights' distance from the ship, saying: "You must stand on that island and keep on beating this drum (Dohol)"[14] (al-Wardi 1922, 147). He agreed and was given food and water which would last him a few days. He headed toward the island and started beating the drum. After a while, he saw the water moving and the ship gradually disappearing from his view. Feeling lonely, the man wandered around the island and observed the largest tree he had ever seen in his life, over which was a thick layer. By the end of the afternoon, the man heard a loud bang and saw the largest bird he had ever seen in his life landing on its nest in the great tree. On the first day, the man hid himself lest the bird should harm him. By early morning, the bird took to the air. When the second night approached, the man came closer to the bird because he felt with helplessness and despair that he had nothing to lose; again, the bird did not harm him. On the third day, the bird was about to fly at dawn, so the man grabbed tightly to its claw (Mot. B 31.1, Type 936A; Mot. B 0542.1.1 & B 0455.6). When he looked down, he only saw the turbulent sea and the Earth becoming small (Mot. F 1021.2.3); he was about to let go due to fatigue but decided to be more patient. Finally, the bird approached the ground and left the man on a small mound of hay in one of the villages while some farmers were watching him. The bird disappeared in the air and the villagers gathered and took him to their leader who understood his language. Everyone was surprised to hear his story, and the man was given plenty of money. After a few days, when he was walking near the beach, he saw his fellows on their ship approaching and they were united again (1980, 88–9). In fact, al-Qazwini's giant tree is an indirect reference to the Tree of Life which is usually associated with the Rukh and the idea of immortality that is discussed above.

However, al-Qazwini does not explain why the drumming of the man made the ship move and so it remains a mystery due to an apparent deletion or distortion of the main tale. However, we can discover more about the story above by consulting a tale from the *Arabian Nights* and some popular practices. In the first voyages of "Sindbad the Seaman and Sindbad the Landsman" (Mot. F 110.3.1) (Burton 1885, vol. vi, 4–14), Sindbad and his fellows were stranded on an island that had trees, but it was in fact a large whale. The giant fish started to move (Mot. B 874) after some sailors lit a fire while others "fell to eating and drinking and playing and sporting." Due to the heat and noise, the whale became agitated and dove into the sea. The captain of the ship was aware of the reality and reacted fast by sailing away and leaving the others. Sindbad was about to drown but was saved by hanging on to a wooden plank and ended up stranded on another island. We learn from Sindbad that there was an island within King Mihrjan's dominions called Kasil "wherein all night is heard the beating of drums and tabrets." Also, Sindbad revealed how he saw a "fish two hundred cubits long," but "the fishermen fear it; so they strike together pieces of wood and put it to flights" (Burton 1885, vol. vi, 11). In Sindbad's Second Voyage, he was thrown to another island where he saw the Rukh bird and its huge egg that looked like a dome; Sindbad tied himself to the bird's talons and was carried by air (Mot. B 522; Type 936A) to a mountain full with diamonds (Mot. F0062). The details mentioned in the first and second voyages bear close resemblance to al-Qazwini's tale mentioned above (Mot. 0963*).

There are other classical accounts of the sea that include similar details. Some merchants were on board a ship that was driven by a strong wind to Dardur. However, the ship's captain, though an old blind man, was experienced in sailing and thought of a way out. He instructed his crew to throw bottles tied to the ship and filled with fat into the sea. After seeing that the fish gathered around the food in the bottles, the captain ordered his men to shout, beat drums, and bang sticks, which greatly frightened the fish so they began to pull the ship out of the dangerous strait. The moment they felt the sea was calm, the captain ordered his crew to cut the ropes and the ship was saved (al-Wardi 1922, 82). Also, a very large fish, probably a whale, was fond of destroying ships in the Gulf of Oman (Mot. B 0877.1.1), so sailors used their drums and made great noise by banging pieces of wood together to scare the fish and drive it away from the ship (al-Ramahirmizi 1908, 15). Finally, Sulaiman al-Tajir and Abi Zaid al-Sirafi (ninth century CE) mentioned that sailors used to use the Christian Naqus (Church Bell) at night to scare the fish, especially the whales (2000, 31). In brief, the use of drums is a technique used by Arab sailors to frighten the whale lest they destroy their ships. In al-Qazwini's tale, the man who started beating the drum was, in fact, trying to make a whale move to enable the ship to sail, too. Hence, the first voyage of Sindbad the sailor and al-Qazwini's tale seem to be closely complementary, for they both shed light on the kind of distortion such tales went through when they were copied by Arab scribes. As mentioned earlier, the habit of beating drums to frighten whales is still rooted in some parts of Arab popular culture whether by the common people or seafarers.

To conclude, the Rukh was molded in the imagination of people in medieval times by combining different descriptions taken from Arabic and Chinese sources, for the Rukh has also indirect associations with the Arab oral tradition. However, there is weak evidence suggesting that the Rukh is directly associated with the Persian Simurgh or the Indian Garuda birds. Instead, the accounts mentioned above of the Arabic "Anqa" bird are closer to the description of the Rukh. All these characteristics are possibly based on the observation of large eagles or other birds that inspired many to narrate tales and draw pictures in order to describe the Rukh's might and grandeur. Further research can be conducted using digital humanities methods to investigate how the Rukh bird was first used in a variety of languages. Since digitized texts offer faster ways to conduct searches, it is far more convenient to conduct comparative literary and folklore studies on relevant corpuses. In this way, more detailed comparisons can be made with other legendary birds like the phoenix, "Anqa," Simurgh, and Garuda in order to better study the minute similarities and differences among them and how they interacted and evolved over time in peoples' imaginations as well as in different cultures and languages. Also, future studies need to investigate how the name of the Rukh bird was first used. What is interesting is the way the Rukh is still depicted in modern Arabic popular culture and oral tradition, especially in children's folktales and cartoons that are largely adapted from the *Arabian Nights* tales. The question that remains is the kind of association and symbolism this bird will carry in the near future.

Notes

1. This chapter is adapted from two previously published papers that appeared in the following journals: Al-Rawi, A. (2017). A Linguistic and Literary Examination of the Rukh Bird in Arab Culture. *Al-'Arabiyya*, vol. 50, pp. 105–117. Al-Rawi, A. (2015). The Rukh and the influence of Chinese mythology. *International Communication of Chinese Culture*, 2, 223–233.
2. There is a misconception that the Rukh is mentioned in Al-Jahidh's *Al-Hayawan* due to Al-Andalusi and Dimiri's reference to Al-Jahidh upon mentioning the Rukh (Al-Dimiri 1978, vol. i: 524). The mistake is probably due to a confusion between two birds: The Rukh and the Rakham (vulture) (Al-Jahidh 1969, vol. iii: 258–9).
3. The editor, Yusif Al-Hadi, mentions that al-Sirafi's work is included in *Masalik Al-Absar* by Ibn Fadhil Al-'Amri.
4. Al-Wardi cites Al-Jawzi's *Kitab Al-Hayawan*, saying that there was an island called Rukh because it contained this bird. Al-Wardi has possibly made a mistake because it is al-Jahidh who has a book called *Al-Hayawan*. Also, Al-Jawzi's only work on zoology is *Iqad' Al-Wasnan bi Ahwal Al-Nabat wa Al-Hayawan*, but Al-Wardi's claim cannot be verified because Al-Jawzi's work is missing now.
5. al-Mas'udi's editor says there is another version of these two works: *Wazrah* and *Shimash* (1973: 260).
6. This is beyond the scope of this study, and I will not attempt to give full details on the "Anqa" here; instead, I will only present relevant information that is related to the Rukh (for more details, see *Encyclopaedia of Islam*, 1997, vol. 1: 509).
7. Bin Hamid's *Dala'l Al-Nubwah* is missing now. It was mentioned though by Ibn Kathir Al-Dimashqi in *Al-Bidayah wa Al-Nihayah* (2003, vol. 9: 35).
8. McElroy observes that in the southern part of Madagascar, "near Isalo, explorers still found the giant eggs of the roc, the great elephant bird" (2001, 25) or Aepyornis, which is believed to be the source of the Rukh's myth.
9. This is a literal translation because the second attribute "Manhuttah" is mainly used to rhyme with "Huttah."
10. al-Wardi cites al-Jawzi's *Kitab al-Haywan*, saying that there was an island called Rukh because it contained this bird. al-Wardi has possibly made a mistake because it is al-Jahidh who has a book called *al-Haywan* 1969. Also, al-Jawzi's only work on zoology is *Iqadh al-Wasnan bi Ahwal al-Nabat wa al-Haywan*, but al-Wardi's claim cannot be verified because al-Jawzi's work is missing now.
11. Arrow-wood is a type of straight tree commonly found in north-eastern China used for making arrows.

12 I identified six books written before al-Qazwini's death which have the same title (Wonders of the Sea), but these are now all lost. The authors are Hisham Bin Mohammed al-Sa'ib Ibn al-Kalbi (Ibn al-Nadim 1978, vol. i, 142; al-Hamawi 1993b, vol. vi, 2781), Şakhar al-Maghribi (Ibn al-Nadim 1978, vol. i, 428), 'Ali Bin Mohammed Bin Shah al-Ţahiri (al-Hamawi 1993b, vol. iv, 1868), Mohammed Bin Ishaq al-Şimiri (al-Hamawi 1993b, vol. vi, 2422), 'Abdullah Bin 'Umru al-Baghdadi, Ibn al-Kawa' (al-Baghdadi 1951, vol. i, 438), and Ibn 'Afawynn (al-Zarkali 2002, vol. vi, 55).

13 This was the name of a strait located between two mountains in the Gulf of Oman; only small ships used to pass it (al-Hamawi 1993a, vol. ii, 450; al-Zubaidi 1998, vol. xi, 287). Because of its location, winds would blow stronger and would create turmoil (whirl) in the sea water (al-Nuweiri 2004, vol. i, 228).

14 The Dohol has two faces and is usually played by using two drumsticks. This drum and other similar ones were and are still used in many Arab countries during the fasting month of Ramadhan. The drummers make their usual noise to wake people up in order to eat before dawn prayer.

References

'S.v. "carcass" & "Rukh"'. In *The Oxford English Dictionary*, 1989.

'Ayssa, Razuq. '"Asil al-'Adah fi Qar" al-Tibul' wa Daq al-Awani al-Nuhasiah fi Khisuff al-Qamar''. *al-Najim* 8 (1936): 49–52.

al-Abi, Mansur Bin al-Hussein. *Nathar al-Durr*. Dar al-Kutub al-'Almyah, 2004.

al-Abshihi, Shihab al-Din. *al-Mustatraf fi fann kull Mustazraf [The Humorous in all the Ludicrous Arts]*. Maktabat al-Jamhuriah al-'Arabiah, 1965.

al-'Alwaji, 'Abdulhamid. 'Qamar Baghdad Bayn Ashdaq al-Hut'. *al-'Iraq al-Jadid* 1 (1962): 4–7.

al-'Ani, 'Abdul 'Aziz. *al-Madinah al-Mughraqah: Dirasah Maidaniah li Madinat Anah*. Dar al-Hurriah lil Tiba'ah, Baghdad: Ministry of Culture and Information, 1985.

Al-'Attar, Farid Al-Din. *Mantiq Al-Tayr*. Dar Al-Andalus lil Tiba'ah wa Al-Nashr, 2002.

al-Ansari, Shamsulldin al-Dimashqi. *Nukhbat al-Dahar fi 'Ajja'ib al-Barr wa al-Bahar*. Otto Harrassowitz, 1923.

Al-'Attar, Farid Al-Din. *Mantiq Al-Tayr*. Edited by Badi' Mohammed Jum'ah (trans.). Beirut: Dar Al-Andalus lil Tiba'ah wa Al-Nashr, 2002.

al-Andulusi, Abi Hamid. *Tuhfat al-Albab wa Nukhbat al-'Ajab*. Beirut: Al Mussasa Al Arabiya lil Dirassat wa Al Nashir, 2003.

al-Attar, Farid al-Din. *Mentiq al-Tayr*. Dar Al-Andalus lil Tiba'ah wa Al-Nashr, 2002.

al-Azhari, Abu Mansur. *Tahdhib al-Lugha*. Dar Ahya' al-Turath al-'Arabi, 2001.

Al-Baghdadi, 'Abdul Qadir Bin Amr. *Khizanat Al-Adab Wa Lub Lubab Lisan Al-Arab*. Cairo: Maktabat Al-Khanji, 1996.

Al-Baghdadi, Isma'il Pasha. *Hidayat Al–'Arifin: Asma' Al-Mu'lifin Wa Athar Al-Musenifin*. Beirut: Dar ahya' Al-Turath Al–'Arabi, 1951.

al-Beiruni, Abu al-Rihan Mohammed. *al-Jamahir fi Ma'rifat al-Jawahir*. 2007.

Al-Brusaui, Isma'il Haqqi. *Tafsir Ruh Al-Bayan*. Constantinople: Matba'ah 'Uthmaniya, 1913.

Al-Dimiri, Kamalulldin. *Hayat Al-Hayawan Al-Kubra*. Cairo: Matba'at Mustafa Al-Babi Al-Halabi, 1978.

Al-Dimashqi, Ibn Kathir. *Al-Bidayah Wa Al-Nihayah*. Beirut: 'Alam Al-Kutub, 2003.

al-Dimiri, Kamalludin bin Musa. *Hayat al-Haywan al-Kubra [The Long Life of the Animal]*. Cairo: Mustafa al-Babwi al-Halab, 1978.
Al-Farahidi, 'Abdul Rahman. *Al-'Ayn*. Beirut: Dar Maktabat Al-Hilal, 1986.
al-Hamawi, Yaqut. *Mu'jam al-Buldan [The Atlas of Countries]*. Vol. 11. Beirut: Sadir, 1993a.
al-Hamawi, Yaqut. *Mu'jam al-Udaba'*. Dar al-Gharb al-Islami, 1993b.
al-Jahidh, Abu 'Uthman. *Al-Hayawan [The Animal]*. Beirut: Dar Ahya' al-Turath al-'Arabi, 1969.
al-Mas'udi, Abu al-Hassan. *Murrujj al-Dhahab wa Ma'adin al-Jawahir*. Dar al-Fikr, 1973.
Al-Nuiri, Shihab Al-Din. *Nihayat Al-'Arb Fi Fanun Al-'Adab*. Beirut: Dar Al-Kutub Al–'Almiya, 2004.
al-Qazwini, Zakarya. *'Aja'ib al-Makhluqat wa Ghara'ib al-Mawjuddat*. Cairo: Mustafa al-alabi, 1980.
al-Ramahirmizi, Buzurg Bin Shahriyar. *Kitab 'Aja'ib al-Hind: Barahu wa Bahrahu wa* Cairo: Dar Al S'adah, 1908.
al-Shahri, 'Ali Ahmed. *Lughat 'Ad. Abu Dhabi: al-Mu'sash al-Wataniah lil Taghlif wa al-Tiba'ah*. Al-Mu'sash al-Wataniah lil Taghlif wa al-Tiba'ah, 2000.
Al-Sirafi, Abi 'Umran Musa. *Al-Sahih min Akhbar Al-Bihar wa 'Aja'ibaha*. Dar Aqra' lil Tiba'ah wa Al-Nashr wa Al-Tawzi', 2006.
Al-Sudani, Abd Al Hasan. *Tribal traditions and values in Amara*. Al Jahidh Publishing, 1990.
al-Tha'alibi, Abi Mansur. *Thimar al-Qulub fi al-Mudaf wa al-Mansub*. Dar al-Ma-arif, 1985.
al-Tajir, Abi Zaid. *Akhbar al-Sin wa al-Hind*. al-Dar al-Masriah al-Lubnaniah, 2000.
al-Tha'labi, Abi Ishaq. *QuSaS al-Anbia' al-Musmma bil 'Arra'is*. Maktabat al-Jamhurriah al-Arabiah, n.d.
Al-Tawhidi, Abu Hayan. *Al-amta' wa Al-Mu'anasah*. Dar Maktabat Al-Hayat lil Tiba'ah wa Al-Nashr, n.d.
al-Wardi, Sirajulldin. *Kharidat al-'aja'ib wa Faridat al-Ghara'ib*. Cairo: Matba'at Mustafa Al-Babi Al-Halabi, 1922.
Al-Zamakhshari, Abi Al-Qasim. *Rabi' al-Abrar wa Nusus al-Akhbar*. Dar Al-'Allami lil Matbu'at, 1992.
al-Zarkali, Khairuddin Bin Mahmud. *al-'Allam*. Dar al-'Alim lil Malayin, 2002.
al-Zubaydi, Mohammed. *Taj 'l-'Arus min Jawahir al-Qamus [The Crown of the Bride from the Gems of the Dictionary]*. Vol. 30. Kuwait: Al-Majlis al-Watani lil Thaqafah wa'l-finun wa'l-A dab, 1998.
Birrell, Anne. *Chinese Mythology: An Introduction*. Baltimore: Johns Hopkins University Press, 1993.
Burton, Richard. *The Book of the Thousand Nights and a Night: A Plain and Literal Translation of The Arabian Nights Entertainments*. London: The Burton Ethnological Society, 1885.
Chauvin, Victor. *Bibliographie Des Ouvrages Arabes Ou Relatifs Aux Arabes Publies Dans l'Europe Chretienne De 1810 a 1885*. Vol. 6. Liege: H. Vaillant-Carmanne, 1902.
Darmesteter, James, ed. (trans.). *The Zend-Avesta Part II*. Oxford: The Clarendon Press, 1883.
Davis, Dick (trans.). *Shahnameh: The Persian Book of Kings*. London: Penguin Books, 2006.

De Gubernatis, Angelo. *Zoological Mythology or the Legends of Animals*, Vol. II. London: Trübner & Company, 1872.

Duyvendak, Jan Julius Lodewijk. 'China's Discovery of Africa: Lectures Given at the University of London on January 22 and 23, 1947'. In *Probsthain's Oriental Series*. London: Arthur Probsthain, 1949.

El-Shamy, H. *Types of the Folktale in the Arab World: A Demographically Oriented Tale-Type Index*. Indiana: Indiana University Press, 2004.

El-Shamy, Hasan. 'Oral Traditional Tales and the Thousand Nights and a Night: The Demographic Factor'. In *The Telling of Stories: Approaches to a Traditional Craft*, edited by Morton Nøjgaard et al., 63–117. Odense: Odense University Press, 1990.

'Encyclopaedia of Islam'. Leiden: E.J. Brill, 1997.

Firdausi. *The Shah Nameh*. Edited by James Atkinson (trans.). London: George Routledge and Sons Limited, 1892.

Giles, Herbert. *Chuang Tzu: Mystic, Moralist, and Social Reformer*. London: Bernard Quaritch, 1889.

Gray, Louis H. 'Fifteen Prakrit-Indo-European Etymologies'. *Journal of the American Oriental Society* 60, no. 3 (1940): 361–69.

Ibn 'Abad, Al-Sahib. *Al-Muhit fi Al-Lugha*.' Alam Al-Kutub, 1994.

Ibn al-Balkhi. *Faris Namah*. al-Dar al-Thaqafiah lil Nashir, 2001.

Ibn, al-Fadhil. *Lisan al-'Arab [The Arabic Tongue]*. Dar Al-Ma'arif, 1981.

Ibn al-Nadim, Abu al-Faraj. *al-Fahrrast*. Dar al-Ma'rrifah, 1978.

Ibn Battutah. *Abi 'Abdullah Mohammed: Rihlat Ibn Battutah*. Al-Matba'ah Al-Khayriya, 1904.

Marzolph, Ulrich, and Richard van Leeuwen. *The Arabian Nights Encyclopedia*. Vol. II. ABC CLIO, 2004.

McElroy, Colleen J. *Over the Lip of the World: Among the Storytellers of Madagascar*. Washington, DC: University of Washington Press, 2001.

Mitra, Kalipadra. 'The Bird and Serpent Myth'. *The Quarterly Journal of the Mythic Society* 16 (1925–6): 189.

New World Private School. 'Sindbad & the Rukh Bird'. 2012. https://www.youtube.com/watch?v=t9PCxV9KdWk.

Polo, Marco. *The Travels of Marco Polo the Venetian*. London: J. M. Dent & Sons LTD, 1914.

Potter, J.W. 'Chinese–East African Trade Before the 16th Century'. *Ufahamu: A Journal of African Studies* 5, no. 2 (1974): 113–34.

Reynolds, Dwight F. *Arab Folklore: A Handbook*. Westport: Greenwood Press, 2007.

West, E.W., ed. (trans.). *Sacred Books of the East*. Vol. 24. Oxford: Oxford University Press, 1885.

Wittkower, Rudolph. '"Roc": An Eastern Prodigy in a Dutch Engraving'. *Journal of the Warburg Institute* 1, no. 3 (1938): 255–57.

YouTube. 2012. 'Sindbad & the Rukh Bird'. Retrieved on 17 May 2016 from https://www.youtube.com/watch?v=t9PCxV9KdWk.

3 The dragon[1]

Introduction

The history of Mesopotamia goes back to more than 5000 BCE when the first towns and cities were built. Mythical beliefs about the creation of the world and man began to spread among the people as part of their basic religious convictions. Among such ideas was the belief in the reality of fearful monsters such as the dragon. In ancient Sumer, the dragon was called Kur and was believed to live deep under the sea. It was said to look like a long serpent that harmed and killed people, so it needed to be slain. The old tales depicted forceful wars between the godly forces of Enki, Ninurta, or Inana and the evil dragon which formed the basis of the Mesopotamian myth of creation (Kramer 1956, 77–83; Jordan 2004, 137–8). In association with Gilgamesh, the legendary Sumerian figure, the dragon was mentioned as an evil and ferocious "serpent" (George 2003, 152). As for the Babylonian and later Assyrian myth of creation, the dragon was called Tiamat which looked like a serpent and was killed by the god Marduk by throwing his arrow into its mouth (Heidel 1963, 83–7; McCall 2001, 52–9). It represented the destructive forces of evil that longed for the seduction of human beings and opposed the heavenly powers of the gods. In other words, the dragon was regarded as the Biblical Satan (Smith 1876, 90–1) and was believed to be an evil and strong creature that created havoc and terrorized its surroundings.

When the Jews of Jerusalem were taken captives in Babylon by Nebuchadnezzar II in the sixth century BCE, they mixed with the people of Mesopotamia and took some of their myths such as that of the dragon, sometimes called Rahab (Rahav), Tanin, Leviathan, or Behemoth. The people of Mesopotamia integrated the dragon into their myth of creation, but in the Old Testament, the Jews introduced another religious dimension to the dragon without altering its physical shape. Jews borrowed the same belief due to their direct contact with the people of Mesopotamia and started using the word "Tannin" which is now the Arabic word for dragon; however, they gave it a distinct Hebrew meaning. The story of the slaying of the dragon Tiamat by Marduk was echoed in the killing of the seven-headed dragon, Leviathan, "the great sea monster," that was found in the Torah (Hooke 2004, 82; *The Jewish Encyclopedia* 1901–6, vol. iv, 648). In the Book of Psalms (104:26), Yahweh manages to subdue the Tannin dragon just like

DOI: 10.4324/9781003462637-3

Marduk. Also, in the Book of Job 40 (7:12), there is a similar image (Day 1985, 74) of slaying a dragon that is presented as a fire-breathing creature.

There are many other Jewish tales about the dragon which borrow the Mesopotamian locale. For example, in the Old Testament Book of Daniel, the tale of Bel, the Dragon, takes place in Babylon (Dalley 1998, 149). In the Prophecy of Daniel (chapter xiv, 16), it is stated that "Then Daniel took pitch, and fat, and hair, and boiled them together: and he made lumps, and put them into the dragon's mouth, and the dragon burst asunder. And he said: Behold him whom you worshipped." This account closely resembles the Babylonian myth of the fight between Marduk and Tiamat (Driver 1900, xx; *The Jewish Encyclopedia* 1901–6, vol. iv, 650–1).

Also, the dragon is said to represent a satanic figure that is punished by God. In the Book of Isaiah (27:1), God is shown as the One to kill the dragon: "the LORD will punish with his sword, his fierce, great and powerful sword, Leviathan the gliding serpent, Leviathan the coiling serpent; he will slay the monster of the sea."

On the other hand, in *The Apocalypse of Abraham* which was allegedly written in the first century CE, the dragon was referred to as Azazel and was regarded as one of God's tools of punishment.[2] In Chapter 31, God promises to punish the sinners, by preparing them to "be food for the fire of Hades," which is another dragon. Most importantly, sinners will be punished "beneath the earth" when they die. "For they shall putrefy in the body of the evil worm Azazel, and be burnt with the fire of Azazel's tongue" (Box 1919, 84–6). Azazel is pictured as a dragon-serpent that stings the sinners in their graves for forsaking God and ignoring His teachings. The same idea is echoed in the Greek Apocryphal of Baruch in which Baruch describes his entry into the third Heaven. In Chapter IV, Baruch asks the Angel about the Dragon and the answer given is: "The Dragon is the one who eats the bodies of those who live wicked lives, and he depends on them for sustenance" (Sparks 1984, 906). James Charlesworth (1983) refers to other old pseudepigrapha Hebrew sources from the first century CE that had references to the dragon such as the "Sibylline Oracles" (the second to the seventh centuries CE) in which the dragon was associated with chaos and was identical with the description found in Revelation 13 (vol. 8, 420). Most of the attributes associated with the dragon that are cited above were later echoed in the Islamic texts of the seventh and eighth centuries CE. In brief, the dragon stood for the evil powers that had to be subdued, but some Jewish texts viewed it as a means of punishment by God against sinners. In the following section, an in-depth analysis is made of some Islamic texts that tackled the dragon in an attempt to understand its origins and nature.

The Islamic dragon

Jews lived in different parts of the Arab world many centuries before the advent of Islam. They had famous Arab tribes such as Himiar, Kindah, Qudha'ah, al-Harith Bin Ka'ab, and Kinanah that played a role in spreading the teachings of

Judaism in the Arabian Peninsula where they resided. Part of their influence was the introduction of several Hebrew stories called the Israiliyyat which later became popular in Islam (Sadan 2004, 44). Another kind of interaction between Arabs before Islam and Judaism is seen in word borrowings. In the Arabic language, the word "Tinnin" refers to the dragon. Etymologically, it is Hebraic because it was in usage several centuries before the Arabic word. Arabs before Islam did not believe in the dragon, and when Islam was introduced into Arabia, Prophet Muhammad stated that the unbelievers would be punished during their "second sleep" in the grave by the "Tinnin" that would bite them continuously until the Day of Judgment. In the Holy Quran, the story of Moses contains an indirect reference to a giant snake that devours other smaller snakes that belong to Egyptian magicians serving the pharaoh.

Based on old Arabic lexicons, the dragon is defined as a kind of serpent (al-Razi 1987, 79; al-Farahidi n.d., vol. viii, 136) and is also known as a great snake (al-Zubaidi 1998, vol. xxxiv, 319) or the greatest of all snakes (Ibn Mandhur n.d., 451; al-Iskafi 1998, vol. ii, 1142). The word has no root in Arabic, which further suggests that it is not originally an Arabic word.

In order to study how Islam viewed the dragon, one must refer to three main sources: the interpretation of the Quran and the prophet's sayings by various Muslim clerics, the Quran itself, and Prophet Muhammad's sayings. In general, the dragon is mainly associated with King Solomon, Prophet Moses, and Alexander the Great. To begin, we need to have a look at some interpretations of selected verses from the Quran.

In surat al-Shu'arra' (The Poets), the story of the Jewish Prophet Moses is narrated (verses 30–50). Moses tries to call upon the followers of the pharaoh to worship God, the one Almighty Being. However, they do not listen and refuse to believe in God; instead, they prefer to worship the pharaoh. As a result, Moses throws his stick on the ground, and it suddenly turns into a huge serpent. According to the Muslim cleric al-Tabari, the serpent raised its head, and it reached one mile high up into the sky. It opened its mouth close to the pharaoh and waited for Moses' orders. However, Moses refrained from killing the pharaoh and agreed to meet him again with the best magicians in Egypt. When the meeting occurred, the magicians presented their magic show, but Moses' serpent came and devoured all the items used by the magicians. Hence, the magicians confessed that Moses' powers far exceeded theirs; they believed in God at once (al-Tabari 2001, vol. ixx, 345–8). The serpent in the story of Moses is similar to the heavenly dragon-serpent that is used to convince the unbelievers to have faith in God. Another Muslim cleric, al-Maqrizi, added other vivid details to the story, saying that when the dragon started producing fire, many people including the pharaoh's daughter were partly burnt. The dragon kept moving and devoured everything in its way such as columns and ropes used to build the pharaoh's palace as well as 200 boats. But the dragon stopped near the palace, opened its jaws, and breathed fire. However, the pharaoh beseeched Moses to stop the dragon, so it turned to other people to devour them. Finally, Moses chided the dragon and caught it, so it turned again to a mere stick (1987, vol. ii, 467).

In relation to Moses and his stick, al-Qurtubi narrated another tale. It is said that the Prophet Shu'ayb inherited a graceful stick from older prophets. Once he gave it to Moses when he drove cattle to a nearby field, but he warned him about the presence of a dragon in the field. Moses did not take heed and preferred to sleep. After a while, the dragon appeared and was about to attack him, yet the stick raised and turned into iron. It fought the dragon until the evil creature died. When Moses woke up, he saw that the stick was covered with blood and a dead dragon lay beside him, so he realized that it was the wondrous work of the stick (1964, vol. xiii, 276–7).

As for King Solomon, he is believed to have been a mighty prophet endowed with unusual riches, strength, and wisdom. For instance, Solomon's golden throne was always referred to in a highly fanciful way. His court contained a couple of eagles, lions, and peacocks that helped Solomon when he sat to read the Torah. A hoard of birds hovered around Solomon and his followers as the throne turned round. It is said that the power behind the rotating throne was a captive dragon (al-Qurtubi 1964, vol. 7, 203). Again, the dragon's power is used to enhance the might of Solomon and adds to the prophet's powers. Interestingly, this description is very close to what is mentioned in the Jewish Testament of Solomon written between the first and fifth centuries CE. The dragon was referred to in Chapter 31 as an apparatus in the service of the heavens: "wilt thou see the heavenly dragons, how they wind themselves along and drag the chariot of the sun" (Ashe 2008, 24). It was believed that the heavenly dragons were a constellation of stars whose task was to turn the sun round the earth, just like the dragon turning Solomon's throne in the Islamic version.

Furthermore, al-Nuweiri mentions the details that preceded the death of King Solomon. He was known to have owned the countries of the East and the West and traveled to all of them. When he reached Qaf Mountain, which was believed to surround the earth, he saw a high wall. He stopped there and asked the wind: "Have you tried to see beyond this wall? The wind said: No, it is the end of the world and only God knows what is beyond it." He ordered the wind to carry him and saw the dragon that looked upon the world. It appeared that the dragon was surrounding the earth and was so huge that it required 500 years to circumambulate (al-Nuweiri 2004, vol. xiv, 107–8). After the death of King Solomon, Oshia succeeded him as a ruler. He had a son called Buluquiya who found a closed tomb in his father's store. The tomb contained an old book that mentioned the name of the coming Prophet Muhammad. So Buluquiya decided to search for the people of Muhammad in order to be guided by them. In his quest, he went to Syria and saw several islands including the two islands of snakes. The snakes said that Hell is filled with them, but the place always boils and bursts with snakes, so they are thrown twice a year to Earth. The snakes' delegate was called Tamlikha. When Buluquiya reached Jerusalem, he met with 'Affan al-Khayr, a Jewish priest, who wanted to catch Tamlikha to gain more powers. Buluquiya agreed and both managed to trap the snake inside a tomb, but they set it free later after getting other magical powers from a tree. The moment it was set free, the snake flew high into the sky and said: "How dare you change God's fate! You'll never get what you desire." The two men went later to fetch Solomon's ring. As Buluquiya was endowed with the magical power of knowing God's greatest name, which is concealed from mankind, he managed to protect himself. Solomon's ring was shielded by a dragon that breathed fire every time a stranger approached Solomon. Buluquiya tried three times to take the ring, but no harm befell him because he said God's name. While Buluquiya was engaged in observing the Archangel Gabriel descending from heaven, the dragon cried so loud that the water on Earth started to boil and earthquakes occurred. As a result, 'Affan fell to the ground and the dragon breathed fire and burnt the man (al-Nuweiri 2004, vol. xiv, 143–6). This story has been adapted by the author(s) of the *Arabian Nights* in "The Adventures of Bulukiya," where we have the same plot and characters (Burton 1885–8, vol. v, 304–28). Tamlikha, the snakes' delegate, becomes Yamlaykha, the queen of serpents. In fact, the story of Bulukiya is mentioned in an old Hebrew scroll (see II Kings 22: 8–13). The texts refer to finding a book that is revered by Jews and that reminds them to be devout to God and His teaching: "our fathers did not obey the stipulations of this book, nor fulfill our written obligations" (Bochman 1996). Another interpretation of this *Arabian Nights* tale says that the Hebrew story of Hilqiya is linked to the epic of Gilgamesh and is close to the Sumerian legend of Inana who traveled to the underworld. In both cases, the serpent-dragon motif is found (Segert 1997, 107; Marzolph and van Leeuwen 2004, 132).

Another chapter in the Holy Quran (surat al-Kahf (verses 93–8)) mentions Alexander the Great and his vast conquests, and some Quran interpreters associate it with the dragon. When Alexander reached the fearful people of Gog and Magog in the Far East, he had to defeat them. They looked like animals but they used to eat grass and feed on beasts. They had long claws and hair that covered all of their bodies (al-Tabari 2001, vol. xviii, 106; al-Nuweiri 2004, vol. xiv, 240). They used to appear along the path located between two mountains in order to destroy cities and kill more people. The residents of the neighboring nations beseeched Alexander to help them, so he built a high wall made of rocks, iron, and copper to prevent Gog and Magog from attacking other people. According to the Islamic tradition, a dragon is thrown every spring to Gog and Magog as a gift from God. They would spend the whole year eating it because of the abundance of meat (al-Tabari 2001, vol. xviii, 106; al-Hamawi n.d., vol. iii, 198). The dragon is thought to be a great serpent that eats all land animals that it sees until it tremendously grows in size. When the other land animals feel too threatened, God sends an angel that carries the dragon to the sea. Then, the dragon, which becomes a sea-serpent, starts eating marine creatures. God then sends another angel that orders the sky clouds to drop and carry the dragon to the people of Gog and Magog (al-Nadim 1978, vol. ii, 585–7; al-Hamawi n.d., vol. iii, 198; al-Qazwini 1980, 96–7 and 99; al-Ramahirmizi 1908, 41–2).

In another story, Alexander the Great was asked by the residents of al-Mastashkin or Dragon Island located in the Caspian Sea to kill a dragon.[3] The island had a high fort and many mountains, rivers, farms, and crops. It is said that the dragon used to eat the people's cattle, so they had to make an offering placed near its den that consisted of two bulls a day. The dragon would devour the two bulls and return to its place. Alexander asked the residents about its location, and he offered two bulls on the first day which were completely eaten the moment the dragon with its glowing eyes approached. On the second day, he asked them to place two thinner cows, so the dragon became hungry on the third day. Alexander ordered the residents to fill two bulls with sulfur, lime, pitch, arsenic, and iron pegs. He placed them in the same spot. When the dragon ate the two bulls, its internal organs were troubled and the pegs got stuck in its mouth. Then, Alexander ordered iron rods to be heated and thrown into the dragon's mouth; thus, the mixture burnt inside the dragon and it died. The residents of the island thanked Alexander for his assistance (al-Idrissi 1989, vol. i, 218–9; al-Wardi 1922, 98–9; al-Nuweiri 2004, vol. xiv, 247; al-Hameiri 1984, vol. i, 166; al-Qazwini 1980, 85). This account is a clear adaptation of the story of Daniel and the slaying of the dragon, mentioned above. Muslim clerics clearly borrowed the story but changed its protagonist.

As for Prophet Muhammad's sayings, the dragon was viewed as one of God's instruments to punish the unbelievers. Before the Day of Judgment, the unbelievers would be punished in the grave in what is called "Grave's Agony." Based on Surat Taha (verse 124), God would send 99 dragons (Tinnins) to all the unbelievers after their death. Each dragon is made up of 99 serpents and each serpent has 7 heads that would sting, scratch, and nibble the corpses until the Day of Resurrection. It is believed that if a dragon breaths fiery air at a spot, no greenery can grow there due to the intense fire produced (Abu al-Fida' 1980, vol. iii, 170; al-Tabari 2001, vol. xxiv, 393–4; al-Haithami 1981, vol. iii, 55; al-Ibshihi 1983, vol. ii, 229). Once, Prophet Muhammad walked into a graveyard where the tombs of the unbelievers from the pre-Islamic era were located. He turned to Bilal, his goodly follower, and told him that the dead were tormented in the grave (al-Haithami 1981, vol. iii, 56). In fact, the description given above is clearly taken from Judaism since it is identical to the older books of the Apocalypse of Abraham and the Greek Apocryphal of Baruch. Besides, the seven-headed dragon is a common description of Leviathan, the Jewish seven-headed dragon (see Revelation 12 (3–4)).[4] However, the new contribution of Islam is to add 99 serpents to the kind of punishment in the grave. According to al-Safuri, the number 99 is used to represent the variant names of God in Islam, and the unbelievers disregarded these sacred names in their worldly lives (2008, vol. i, 80). In the following section, a detailed discussion is given on the other varying accounts of the dragon in different Arabic writings.

The Judeo-Christian dragon of Arabia

In order to further understand the different dimensions of the dragon in Arabia, it is important to mention what other Arab writers in the fields of geography, history, and sciences have said about it. Lutz Röhrich (2003) asserts that the dragon is usually perceived as having two different forms: a large snake or a combination of a crocodile and predatory bird (vol. 3, 787–820). This is true of the other popular descriptions of the dragon in Arabic sources that do not discuss Islamic theology as will be discussed below. What is striking is that most of the following accounts involve places with Christian gatherings especially in and around Antioch which may partly explain the origins of the other beliefs in the dragon. For instance, al-Qazwini says that dragons usually appear in places near Antioch such as Tripoli, Latakia, and Mount Halak (1980, 95). al-Jahidh and al-Isfahani agreed that it was only the people of al-Sham (modern Palestine, Syria, Jordan, and Lebanon) and Antioch who narrated stories of sea dragons breathing fire like thunderstorms and burning everything in their way (al-Jahidh 1969, vol. iv, 154; al-Isfahani 2004, vol. iv, 782). This clearly shows that myths live with the people who believe in them. For instance, many crusaders in the twelfth century believed that St. George fought the dragon. Incidentally, the alleged fight took place in the Middle East, and the dragon's appearance looked similar to the Sumerian dragon which suggests that the European (Christian) dragon had Middle Eastern and in particular Mesopotamian origins (Kramer 1956, 196).

The Arab historian al-Hamawi referred to a story that spread in Aleppo, Syria, in the year 1292. He said that many people saw in Kalaz near Antioch a great dragon that was as high and thick as a minaret and that fire was coming out of its mouth and tail. It burnt everything it came close to such as houses and their residents, including women and children. People became very frightened, so God sent a cloud that carried the dragon up into the sky while fire was still being released from its mouth and tail. More than 500 olive and almond trees were burnt because of this dragon (n.d., vol. iv, 476). Another story narrated by al-Hamawi is about al-Musaisah near Tarsus in modern Turkey. He said that a friend heard people talking about how the sea remained turbulent and noisy for several days. So people thought that the marine animals were crying to God for rescue. All of a sudden, seven clouds dropped and carried the dragon from the Antioch Sea. As it was lifted, it hit with its tail tens of Antioch's wall towers. People believed that dragons never raise their heads above the surface of the sea lest the clouds snatch them (n.d., vol. iii, 198). Also, Ibn Kathir, another Arab historian, mentioned that in one of the villages of Damascus, a fearful dragon appeared in the year 1294 and devoured a very big goat (Ibn Kathir 1988, vol. xiii, 396). In addition, al-Jahidh described another dragon that appeared in Antioch. Some people said that the upper part of Antioch's minaret looked different from the rest of its remaining structure. The people believed that a dragon raised itself one day from the sea and flew over the city, so it blew the minaret with its tail and destroyed that part. The residents of the city restored it later (1969, vol. iv, 154).

Another popular tale linked to Christianity is the story of Fymiun from Najran in Yemen. The residents of Najran were Christians before Islam due to the mysterious figure of Fymiun who was known to have performed miracles like curing people from their diseases. He was reputed to be a pious and independent person because he refused to rely on others to earn his living. He had an admirer from al-Sham called Salih who loved to follow him wherever he went. One day, Fymiun headed toward the wilderness to pray while Salih observed from afar. As Fymiun was praying, a dragon appeared and was about to devour him. In the meantime, Salih cried loudly to warn Fymiun about the dangerous dragon, but the latter did not pay attention. As the dragon came close to Fymiun, it died all of a sudden. When the people of Najran heard the story, they were astonished so they decided to convert to Christianity (al-Tabari 1986, vol. i, 434; al-Hamawi n.d., vol. v, 266; Abdullmalik, Bin Hisham 1990, vol. i, 146–7).

In relation to dragon offerings, there was in Tai'f (modern-day Saudi Arabia) an old fort built before Islam. It had a well and it was believed that a dragon dwelt in it and prevented anyone from building near the fort unless people made an offering (Ibn al-Dhia' n.d., vol. i, 159). Noteworthy, Tai'f was populated with Jews from Yemen before the advent of Islam ('Ali 2001, vol. vii, 147), and, probably, the idea was introduced to the pagan Arabs by them. However, this story has many similarities to the Christian legend of St. George and the slaying of the Dragon.[5] Hence, the source of such a belief is not clear.

Other popular convictions are worth mentioning. For instance, the dragon is described as being as long as a high palm tree; its body is black like the night, and its eyes are red with a very bright glittering. Above all, it has a very ugly shape (al-Ibshihi 1983, vol. ii, 228; al-Qazwini 1980, 86 and 87). Abi Hamid al-Andulusi (c. 1169 d.) believed that there was a certain kind of fish called Tinnin which was black in color, long like a serpent, and had red eyes and teeth as sharp as spears. It was stronger and more violent and aggressive than the shark. The shark was said to run away from the Tinnin upon seeing it. It was believed that the Tinnin would appear from the sea and devour every human it saw on the beach. If it was caught when still young, fishermen would kill it, and its meat given to those who suffer from palsy or cold due to the warming effect of its meat (al-Andulusi 2003, 74). It was also believed that if there was a scarcity of water and the creature remained in the mud for six hours, it would become restless and two wings would appear from underneath its skin, and it would fly to the deep sea. According to eyewitnesses, the length of the dragon was about six miles; its color resembled that of a tiger, its scales like fish, its head looked human but was as big as a mountain, and its wings were great and looked like those of fish. It had two long ears and very big circular eyes. Also, it had six other smaller necks; each one was about ten meters long, and their heads looked like snakes (al-Qazwini 1980, 99). Interestingly, al-Qazwini mentions a unique dragon recipe. It is said that dragon's meat if eaten produces bravery. Also, if a dragon's blood is used to cover a man's penis before sexual intercourse, his partner would experience great ecstasy (ibid.). The description given here looks closer to the Babylonian inscriptions found in the remains of ancient sites, which suggests that Arabs visualized this creature based on the engravings left by older civilizations.

Finally, many Arabic oral tales, which are considered the crucible of popular thought, involved dragons in their plots. Hasan El-Shamy refers to tens of such tales with tale-types such as 0300 (the dragon-slayer), 0312D (brother saves his sister and brothers from the dragon), and 0466** (the journey to hell; the hero rescues three maidens from the dragon). The popular dragon motifs were T0172.2 (bridal chamber invaded by a magic dragon (serpent)), B11.10 (sacrifice of a human being to a dragon), and B11.11 (fight with a dragon) (El-Shamy 2004, 999–1000). This shows that the dragon myth became fully integrated into Arabic-Islamic culture and society and constituted an important element in the imagination of story tellers. Yet, the contemporary view of the dragon among Arabs is mostly taken from the Hebrew dragon.

In conclusion, Judaism and Christianity surely popularized the dragon myth in Arabia. Many people started imagining dragons in clouds that take unique shapes. When hurricanes or tornadoes hit cities and cause havoc, people thought it was the force of the dragon's tail that lifted animals into the sky and destroyed buildings. When the seawater was turbulent, a dragon was thought to be moving. If a whale passed, it was viewed as a furious dragon. If people witnessed a sheep or a calf devoured by a large python, they saw it as a dragon. Also, the Jewish myth that dragons sting and bite the dead probably originated because this was how ancient people interpreted the natural blood clotting and bloating that occur when corpses decompose. However, it is important to note that not all Arab Muslims believed in the Judeo-Christian dragon. al-Jahidh, for instance, who belonged to the intellectual school of Mu'tazilah, doubted the reality of the dragon and confirmed that many people negated its very existence. He confessed that the belief in the dragon was baseless just like the belief in the 'Anqa,' a phoenix-like legendary bird (al-Jahidh 1969, vol. iv, 155 and vol. vii, 105).

In all cases, the Islamic dragon "Tinnin" is basically taken from the Hebrew dragon, so it is the descendant of the Babylonian dragon, Tiamat. It was generally viewed as God's instrument to punish unbelievers, but it is also linked to other mythical beings like Gog and Magog. Muslim clerics made use of Hebrew tales in interpreting some chapters from the Holy Quran. Most importantly, Islam associated 99 serpents with the dragon which distinguished it from other popular dragons. Further studies on the Islamic Tinnin and the dragon of Arabia need to be conducted to investigate how and which dragon preoccupied Arab literary writers in modern times and to what effect.

Notes

1 The content of this chapter has previously appeared as a research paper published in the following journal: Al-Rawi, A. K. (2012). The Religious Connotation of the Islamic Dragon. *Fabula*, 53(1–2), 82–93.
2 In fact, the name "Azazel" is closer to the Islamic Angel of Death 'Azra'il.
3 al-Qazwini says that the island is located in the Persian Sea instead.
4 "And there appeared another wonder in heaven; and behold a great red dragon, having seven heads and ten horns, and seven crowns upon his heads. And his tail drew the third part of the stars of heaven, and did cast them to the earth: and the dragon stood before the woman which was ready to be delivered, for to devour her child as soon as it was born."

5 For more information on St. George and the Dragon, see J.F. Campbell's *The Celtic Dragon Myth*. New York 2004.

References

'Ali, Jawad. *Al-Mufassal Fi Tarikh al-'Arab Qabla al-Islam*. London: Dar Al Saqi, 2001.

Abdullmalik, Bin Hisham. *Al-Syrah al-Nabawyah*. Beirut: Dar Al Kitab Al-Arabi, 1990.

Abu al-Fida', Isma 'il Bin 'Omar. *Tafsir Ibn Kathir*. Vol. i. Beirut: Dar Al-Kutub Al-Almiah, 1980.

al-Andulusi, Abi Hamid. *Tuhfat al-Albab wa Nukhbat al-'Ajab*. Beirut: Al Mussasa Al Arabiya lil Dirassat wa Al Nashir, 2003.

al-Farahidi, Abu 'Abdulrahman. *Kitab al- 'Ayen*. Cairo: Dar Al Hilal, n.d.

al-Haithami, 'Ali Ibn Abi Bakr. *Majma' al-Zawa'id wa Manba' al-Fawa'id*. Beirut: Dar Al Kitab, 1981.

al-Hamawi, Yaqut. *Mu'jam al-Buldan [The Atlas of Countries]*. Al Shamila E-book, n.d.

al-Hameiri, Mohammed. *al-Roudh al-Mi'tar fi Khabar al-Aqtar*. Beirut: Maktabat Lebanon, 1984.

al-Ibshihi, Shihabulldin. *al-Mustatraf fi fenn Kull Mustadraf*. Cairo: Dar Al Kutub Al A'limiah Lil Nashir, 1983.

al-Idrissi, Abu 'Abd Mohammed. *Nuzhat al-Mishtaq fi Ikhtraq al-Afaq*. Riadh: A'lam Al Kutub Lil Tiba'ah wa Al Tawzeea, 1989.

al-Isfahani, al-Raghib. *Muhaharat al-Udaba' wa Muhawarat al-Shu'ra' wa al-bulagha'*. Vol. i. Beirut: Dar Sadir, 2004.

al-Iskafi, Abu Abdullah. *Mukhtasar Kitab al-'Ayn [The Shortened Book of the "Well"]*. Vol. 2. Muscat: Ministry of National Heritage and Culture, 1998.

al-Jahidh, Abu 'Uthman. *Al-Hayawan [The Animal]*. Beirut: Dar Ahya' al-Turath al-'Arabi, 1969.

al-Maqrizi, Taqi al-Deen. *al-Mawa'idh wa al-I'tibar Bidhkr al-Khutat wa Athar*. Cairo: Miktabat Al Thaqafa Al Deenya, 1987.

al-Nadim, Mohammed Bin Ishaq. *al-Fahras*. Beirut: Dar Al Mi'rifah, 1978.

Al-Nuweiri, Shihab Al-Din. *Nihayat Al-'Arb Fi Fanun Al-'Adab*. Beirut: Dar Al-Kutub Al-'Almiya, 2004.

al-Qazwini, Zakarya. *'Aja'ib al-Makhluqat wa Ghara'ib al-Mawjuddat*. Cairo: Mustafa al-alabi, 1980.

al-Qurtubi, Abu'Abdullah Mohammed. *Tafsir al-Qurtubi*. Vol. xv. Cairo: Dar al-Sha'ab, 1964.

al-Ramahirmizi, Buzurg Bin Shahriyar. *Kitab 'Aja'ib al-Hind: Barahu wa Bahrahu wa Jaza'irahu*. Cairo: Dar Al S'adah, 1908.

al-Razi, Mohammed Bin Abi Bakr. *Mukhtar al-Sahah*. Beirut: Dar Al Jeel, 1987.

al-Safuri, 'Abdul-rahman. *Nuzhat al-Majalis wa Muntakhab al-Nafa'is*. Al-Shamela e-book, 2008.

al-Tabari, Mohammed Bin Jarir. *Jami' al-Bayan fi Ta'wil al-Quran*. Cairo: Dar Hajjir, 2001.

al-Tabari, Mohammed Bin Jarir. *Ta'rrikh al-Tabari*. Cairo: Dar Al Ma'arif, 1986.

al-Wardi, Sirajulldin. *Kharidat al-'aja'ib wa Faridat al-Ghara'ib*. Cairo: Matba'at Mustafa Al-Babi Al-Halabi, 1922.

al-Zubaidi, Mohammed. *Taj 'l-'Arus min Jawahir al-Qamus [The Crown of the Bride from the Gems of the Dictionary]*. Vol. 30. Kuwait: Al-Majlis al-Watani lil Thaqafah wa'l-finun wa'l-Adab, 1998.

Ashe, Steven. *Qabalah– The Testament of Solomon– The Wisdom of Solomon*. Somerset: Glastonbury Books, 2008.

Bochman, Victor. 'The Jews and "The Arabian Nights".' *The Israel Review of Arts and Letters* 103 (1996), 39–47.

Box, G.H. (trans.). *The Apocalypse of Abraham*. London: The Macmillan Company, 1919.

Burton, Richard F. *The Book of the Thousand Nights and a Night: With Introduction Explanatory Notes on the Manners and Customs of Moslem Men and a Terminal Essay Upon the History of the Nights*. London: The Burton Club, 1885–8.

Charlesworth, James H., ed. *The Old Testament Pseudepigrapha: Apocalyptic Literature and Testaments*. London: Doubleday, 1983.

Dalley, Stephanie. *The Legacy of Mesopotamia*. Oxford: Oxford University Press, 1998.

Day, John. *God's Conflict with the Dragon and the Sea: Echoes of a Canaanite Myth in the Old Testament*. Cambridge: Cambridge University Press, 1985.

Driver, S.R. *The Book of Daniel*. Cambridge: Cambridge University Press, 1900.

El-Shamy, Hasan. *Types of the Folktale in the Arab World: A Demographically Oriented Tale-Type Index*. Bloomington: Indiana University Press, 2004.

George, Andrew. *The Epic of Gilgamesh: The Babylonian Epic Poem and Other Texts in Akkadian and Sumerian*. London: Folio Society, 2003.

Heidel, Alexander. *The Babylonian Genesis: The Story of Creation*. Chicago: University of Chicago Press, 1963.

Hooke, S.H. *Middle Eastern Mythology*. New York: Dover Publications Inc., 2004.

Ibn al-Dhia', Abi al-Baqa'. *Tarikh Mecca al-Musharafah wa al-Masjid al-Haram*. Al-warraq e-book, n.d.

Ibn Kathir, Abi Al-Fida'. *Al-Bidayah Wa al-Nihayah*. Beirut: Dar Ahia'a Al Turath Al Arabi, 1988.

Ibn Mandhur, Mohammed Bin Makram. *Lissan Al-'Arab*. Cairo: Dar Al Ma'arif, n.d.

Jordan, Michael. *Dictionary of Gods and Goddesses*. New York: Facts On File. Inc., 2004.

Kramer, Samuel Noah. *Sumerian Mythology: A Study of Spiritual and Literary Achievement in the Third Millennium BC*. Indian Hills: Falcon's Wing Press, 1961.

Kramer, Samuel Noah. *From the Tablets of Sumer: Twenty-Five Firsts in Man's Recorded History*. Indian Hills: Falcon's Wing Press, 1956.

Marzolph, Ulrich, and Richard van Leeuwen, eds. *The Arabian Nights Encyclopedia*. Santa Barbara: ABC-CLIO, Inc., 2004.

McCall, Henrietta: *Mesopotamian Myths*. Texas: University of Texas Press, 2001.

Röhrich, Lutz. 'Dragon'. *Enzyklopädie Des Märchens*. Berlin: Walter de Gruyter, 3 (2003): 787–820.

Sadan, Joseph. 'The Arabian Nights and the Jews'. In *The Arabian Nights Encyclopedia*, edited by Ulrich Marzolph and Richard van Leeuwen. Santa Barbara: ABC-CLIO, Inc., 42–46, 2004.

Segert, Stanislav. 'Ancient Near Eastern Traditions in The Thousand and One Nights'. In *The Thousand and One Nights in Arabic Literature and Society*, edited by Richard Hovannisian and Georges Sabagh, 106–13. Cambridge: Cambridge University Press, 1997.

Smith, George. *The Chaldean Account of Genesis*. New York: Scribner, Armstrong & Co., 1876.

Sparks, Hedley Davis, ed. *The Apocryphal Old Testament*. Oxford: Oxford University Press, 1984.

The Jewish Encyclopedia. *Dragon*. Vol. 4. New York: Funk & Wagnalls Company, 1901–1906.

Conclusion

This manuscript explores the belief in and perception of a number of supernatural creatures that are still popular in some parts of the Arab region and around the world. Some of these creatures are still culturally visible today. We find, for example, representations of the dragon and Rukh in children's folktales and cartoons as well as the ghoul's persistent presence in films, video games, and stories, with Galland's influence still lurking especially in Western countries. In almost all Arab countries, the ghoul is viewed as a monster that eats human beings and is used as a means of instilling fear inside children's hearts. Many modern stories rewritten and adapted from old Arabic folktales deal with this monster, whose description resembles that mentioned in this work. For example, the Palestinian writer Amil Habibi published a story called "Saraya Bint al-Ghoul" dealing with a girl called Saraya who was kidnapped by a ghoul and was imprisoned in his palace. Later, her cousin searched for her and managed to rescue her (Motif G0440.1 "ogre abducts woman (maiden)" and motif G0500 "ogre defeated") (El-Shamy 2004, 1073–4). Another Palestinian, Jamil al-Salhut, published a story for children called "al-Ghoul" portraying a small girl called Khadijah who dreamt of the ghoul after hearing a horrible description of it from her grandmother, so she urinated while asleep due to her excessive fear. When she told the dream to her teacher at school, the grandmother was criticized for telling such old legends. Furthermore, the famous Egyptian film actor ʻAdil Imam starred in *al-Ghoul* (1981) in which he appeared as a journalist trying to discover the truth about a fearful and cruel tycoon who harmed people and exploited them. The ghoul in this film referred to a hideous person due to his ugly behavior, as is the case in old Arabic proverbs. I argue that Islam accepted the beliefs in pre-Islamic ghouls and genies due to their strong relevance and connection to Arab culture and its literary tradition.

In the first chapter, I presented the conceptual development of the ghoul creature and how some *Arabian Nights* tales had similar motifs and plots to older writings in Arabic literary traditions. I then traced the creature's transformation in the Western world due to Antoine Galland's translation of the *Nights*, by showing how terms such as "ogre" and "ogress" were employed in Western folktales as vampire creatures to substitute for the Arabic ghoul.

DOI: 10.4324/9781003462637-4

I also argued that Charles Perrault's *Le Petit Poucet* folktale prototype was potentially influenced by a similar Arabic story. Finally, Arab Bedouins remain crucial in maintaining belief in the ghoul since they remain slightly secluded from the impact of globalization.

In the second chapter, I discussed the supernatural Rukh bird. Once again, the *Arabian Nights* played an important role in introducing this legendary creature into the Western world in addition to Marco Polo's travel writing. According to Arabic sources, the Rukh is a huge bird that lives close to China in isolated and remote islands. I argue that there are Chinese cultural influences shaping the supernatural belief in this creature, and it has a strong link to the Arabic "Anqa" bird. However, a few other scholarly accounts associate the Rukh with the Indian Garuda or the Persian Simurgh birds, yet their descriptions and features differ in many ways, especially in relation to the Rukh's distinctive Islamic and Arabic elements and its connection to Chinese mythology.

Finally, the third chapter explores the Islamic dragon, the Tinnin, and I argue that it has strong historical origins in Mesopotamian mythology and Hebrew texts. Due to their geographical proximity, Islam borrowed the belief in this supernatural creature from Judaism which in turn adapted it from Sumerian and Babylonian legends of the Tiamat, depicted as a terrifying serpent which often floats on the river.

There is no doubt that these supernatural creatures preoccupied people's minds and imaginations for thousands of years as many imagined seeing them on the moon, clouds, and in the waters, often taking unique faces and shapes. When natural phenomena like storms and floods occurred, some people imagined these creatures such as the dragon or the Rukh were responsible for causing them, especially when scientific explanations were not found. For example, and in view of the details given in Chapter 1, ghouls may have merely been real human beings carrying some birth defects. The mouth of the ghoul is believed to have the shape of a cat's, or what is now medically called a "cleft lip" and "cleft palate." In addition, a ghoul is thought to have deformed legs or hands that look like that of an ass, a description similar to the medical condition "ankylodactylia," and it has hair covering a great deal of its body. In fact, many children around the world are born with such features every year due to environmental factors and/or genetic mutations (Carinci et al. 2007, 2). If one takes into account the fact that pregnant women in the desert lack basic nutritious food and that many Arabs, to this very day, commonly practice intermarriage within their own tribes over many generations, one can conclude that the ghoul may possibly be a child with some birth defects. After giving birth, the mother might be forced to part with her child due to their congenital birth deformities. As a result, the child would be ostracized from their tribe and would seek the desert as a refuge due to the important role superstitions played in the lives of Arabs before Islam. In medieval Europe, for example, a child born with a mental or physical disorder was mainly "viewed as evil." When Martin Luther heard about such a child, he recommended that he "be disposed of by drowning" (Eberly 1991, 228, 231). In a medical study conducted on Nigerian women giving birth to children suffering from cleft lips and palate, 7 out of 16 women interviewed from the Yoruba ethnic group believed that "evil spirits" were behind their children's birth defects. Eight of those women considered spiritual healing the only method of treatment (Olasoji Ugboko and Arotiba 2007, 304). Hence, the Arabic stories that mention a marriage taking place between a human being and a si'lwah may be true if we consider the abovementioned assumption. In other words, the ghoul could be a real human being born with some birth defects, compelling them to reside in the wilderness to avoid other humans who would naturally loathe and fear these individuals.

To sum up, the supernatural creatures examined here in this manuscript have preoccupied Arabs for several centuries and will certainly remain a source of inspiration for many readers around the world as well as a cause of fear for many children. One of the main reasons behind their fearful character is their mysterious nature as there is no unified agreement about their features. The ghoul in the Arab region, for example, continues to be a kind of devil, genie, enchantress of genies, devilish genie, and spirit. However, most accounts mention this monster as an ugly and harmful female creature. The belief in such a supernatural being is still solid, for ghoulish tales remain popular. What is striking is that these supernatural beings refuse to fade away from the imagination of some people regardless of the passage of time and the various world cultures they have encountered.

My hope is that this manuscript encourages other interested scholars to delve into the historical development and cultural significance of other legends, myths, and superstitions in the Arab region and elsewhere, for there are hundreds of other supernatural creatures that still need to be carefully studied and analyzed using a variety of sources and research methods. For example, future research can employ computational and digital humanities approaches to examine how other supernatural creatures first emerged in different languages, allowing a more efficient way to conduct comparative folklore studies.

References

Carinci, Francesco, Luca Scapoli, Annalisa Palmieri, Ilaria Zollino, and Furio Pezzetti. 'Human Genetic Factors in Non-Syndromic Cleft Lip and Palate: An Update'. *International Journal of Pediatric Otorhinolaryngology* 10, no. 1016 (2007): 1–11.

Eberly, Susan Schoon. 'Fairies and the Folklore of Disability: Changelings, Hybrids, and the Solitary Fairy'. In *The Good People: New Fairylore Essays*, edited by Peter Narváez, 227–50. Kentucky: The University Press of Kentucky, 1991.

El-Shamy, H. *Types of the Folktale in the Arab World: A Demographically Oriented Tale-Type Index*. Indiana: Indiana University Press, 2004.

Olasoji, H.O., V.I. Ugboko, and G.T. Arotiba. 'Cultural and Religious Components in Nigerian Parents' Perceptions of the Aetiology of Cleft Lip and Palate: Implications for Treatment and Rehabilitation'. *British Journal of Oral and Maxillofacial Surgery* 45 (2007): 302–5.

Index

For Product Safety Concerns and Information please contact our EU representative GPSR@taylorandfrancis.com
Taylor & Francis Verlag GmbH, Kaufingerstraße 24, 80331 München, Germany

www.ingramcontent.com/pod-product-compliance
Lightning Source LLC
LaVergne TN
LVHW010939110826
845149LV00013B/2678

* 9 7 8 1 0 3 2 6 1 2 2 5 6 *